DERBYSHIRE
THROUGH TIME

Margaret Buxton

AMBERLEY PUBLISHING

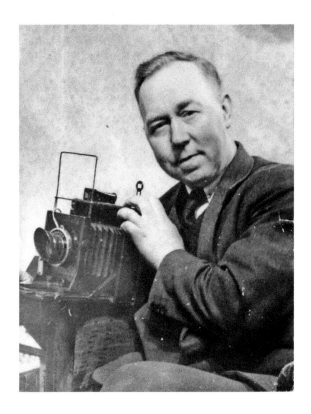

First published 2009

Amberley Publishing Plc
Cirencester Road, Chalford,
Stroud, Gloucestershire, GL6 8PE

www.amberley-books.com

British Library Cataloguing in Publication Data.
A catalogue record for this book is available from the British Library.

ISBN 978 1 84868 517 8

Typesetting and Origination by Amberley Publishing.
Printed in Great Britain.

Acknowledgements

As was the case in my previous five books, this work has only been possible because of photographs taken by my Father, Harry Buxton (1908-1983). He was born in Hadfield and – other than a few of his childhood years spent in Manchester – he lived all his life in Glossopdale and in the High Peak of Derbyshire.

Being a keen photographer from the age of seven, at first amateur and later professionally, he took so many photographs during his life that I, his daughter, have been able to share some of them in my books. Over the years he used many kinds of cameras, at first fitted with glass plates and later with films. He used large flash bulbs and heavy electronic flash-guns. Long before the use of digital cameras and computer enhancements, he processed and printed all his own work using chemicals and large equipment in his darkroom at home. Many were newsworthy photographs and some, at the time, were quite ordinary everyday shots of people and scenes. These pictures have now become an historical record of bygone times and with their modern day comparatives, which I have endeavoured to depict, the reader will better appreciate the changes that time has wrought in this part of Derbyshire. After retirement, he served the borough as a local councillor and gave many slide shows.

As I write these lines it is 100 years since his birth, although a Blue Plaque in his memory would be wonderful, I hope this book is a fitting tribute to the man who never left home without a camera and had the foresight to capture so much of our ever-changing world.

Margaret Buxton, 2009

Introduction

This book looks at locations in the north-west of Derbyshire. Some pictures are taken in the Peak District National Park, of which Derbyshire was the first in Britain in 1951, covering 542 square miles over six counties. The Northern part is known as the Dark Peak and it is the highest land consisting of moorland and reservoirs. The Southern parts are called the White Peak, after the limestone that dominates the landscape. It is here that the lovely dales or valleys are found.

The highest peak, at 2,088ft, is Kinder Scout, which was the scene of the famous Mass Trespass in the thirties. Parts of the 256 mile-long Pennine Way path and 210 mile-long Trans Pennine Trail fall within the county's boundary and are very popular places for cyclists, horse riders and ramblers. Bleaklow Hill, in Glossopdale, was the backdrop for the television location Royston Vasey and the neighbouring moorland has been the scene of several air crashes.

Many houses in the region are built of stone and the villages celebrate wonderful festivals and hold interesting community events. The ancient custom of well dressing, dating from Celtic times, was originally only found in or around the borders of Derbyshire. The villages of Derwent and Howden disappeared under the Ladybower reservoir and the 617 Dambuster Squadron trained over these waters. Other reservoirs are feeders to canals or supply drinking water to people outside the region. Ancient railways and canal basins all have interesting stories to tell. Castleton's caverns are the only place from which the Blue John Stone is mined and many examples of it grace palaces around the world. Crich is the home of the National Tramway Museum

The Dukes of Devonshire, the Dukes of Norfolk and the National Trust have all been landowners in the county and treasures like Chatsworth House and Haddon Hall attract thousands of visitors each year. Not far away is the village of Eyam, noted for the Great Plague. Anne Boleyn was the grandchild of one of the Duke's of Norfolk. Betty Driver from Coronation Street and the musician Syd Lawrence once owned pubs in Whaley Bridge and the White

Hart, in the same village, was featured in *The Manchester Man*. Vera Brittain, author of *Testament of Youth*, lived in the Spa town of Buxton, whose Opera House attracts many top class performances.

Some of the films and television series that have been located in Derbyshire include *Peak Practice*, *Pride & Prejudice*, *Elizabeth*, *The Other Boleyn Girl*, *Jane Eyre*, *Moll Flanders*, *Prince & the Pauper*, *Sense & Sensibility*, *Chronicles of Narnia*, *Far from the Madding Crowd*, *Sons and Lovers*, *League of Gentlemen*, *Stig of the Dump* and *Anne Boleyn*. Parts of Derbyshire have changed to keep abreast with modern times, but still there are areas that manage to retain a charm that is timeless.

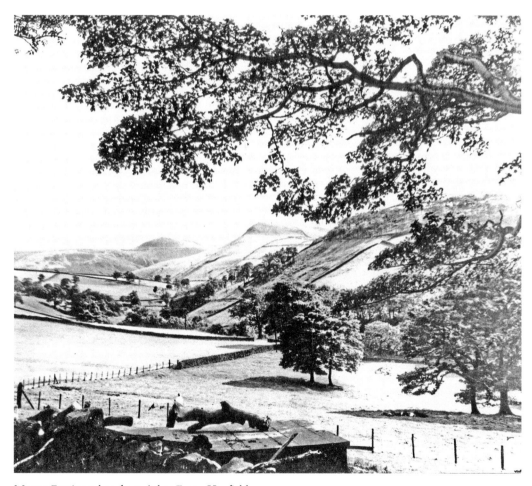

Mount Famine taken from Ashes Farm, Hayfield.

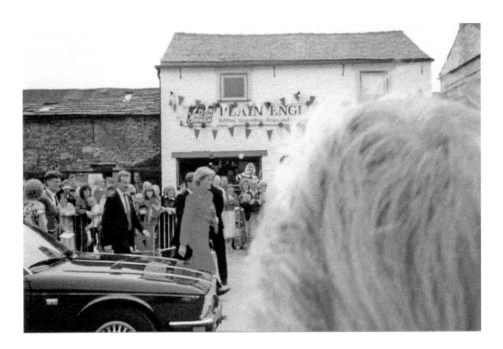

Canal Street

On her visit to the High Peak in Derbyshire in 1990, Princess Diana stopped at the canal basin in Whaley Bridge. Just prior to this scene, a lady in the crowd asked her, 'how are the children?' and her witty reply was, 'All three are fine!' The building in Canal Street, decorated in her honour, was used as a base for the Plain English Campaign, whose aim is to get companies and the legal profession to use less jargon in their documents. Now, they are based in the village of New Mills. Outram House has become home to the owners of the canal boat *Judith Mary* and includes a gift and flower shop.

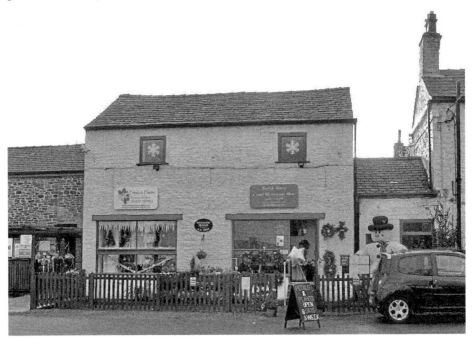

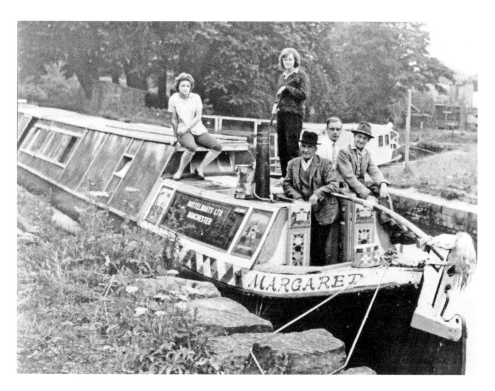

Canal Basin, Whaley Bridge

In 1962 this horse-drawn boat *Margaret* stopped at the canal basin on its 109 mile cruise. Today the 72ft long restaurant boat *Judith Mary* moors here. Close to the footbridge there is a sluice point for the many narrow boats that visit here and Bingswood Industrial Estate is in the distance. To the right of the moorings the Transhipment Shed, built in 1832, is a Grade 11 listed warehouse where the Peak Forest Canal became a transfer point with the Cromford & High Peak Railway to unload coal and limestone. The East Midland Development Agency has awarded money for the warehouse restoration.

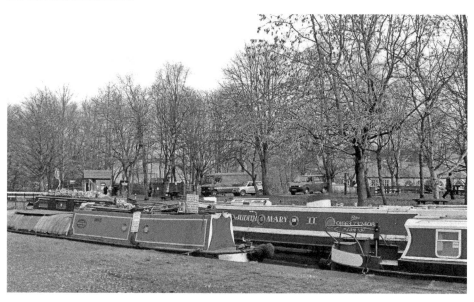

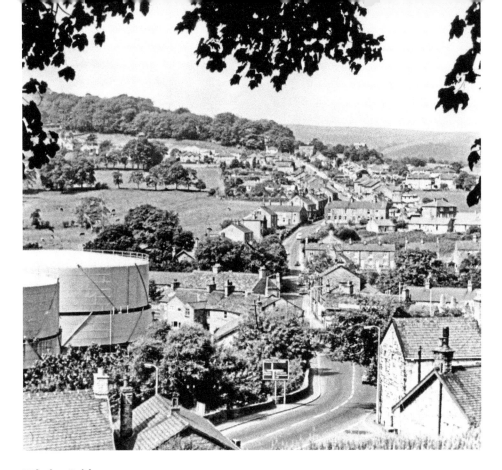

Whaley Bridge

The name Whaley Bridge comes from the ancient crossing place of the River Goyt. Used by the Romans it is twinned with Tymbark in Poland. In 1866, Whaley Bridge Gas Company charged the town 34s to light the town's nine street lamps and £2 12s per year for lighting, cleaning and extinguishing them. From Rock Bank, off Chapel Road in Horwich End, the old gasworks was still visible before demolition. Smaller signs at the road end and in the distance have replaced the directional sign to Buxton, Macclesfield, Stockport and Manchester, and the view is dominated by the white roofed building of MPE Company.

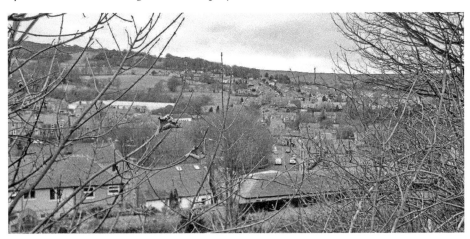

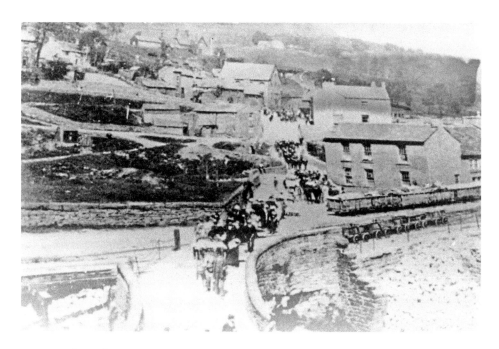

Bugsworth Basin

Bugsworth Basin, the terminus of the Peak Forest Canal, closed in 1927. Benjamin Outram built the 14.5 mile-long canal in 1795-6 from Portland Basin in Ashton-Under-Lyne. Tramways brought limestone from Lodes Knowle and Dove Holes quarries for transhipment into canal boats. The loaded wagons moved down the tramway using gravity and the empty wagons were then hauled back by horses. Pat Phoenix, who played the part of Elsie Tanner in television's *Coronation Street*, once owned the Navigation Inn on the right.

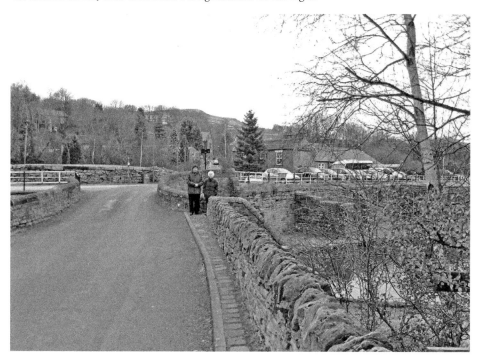

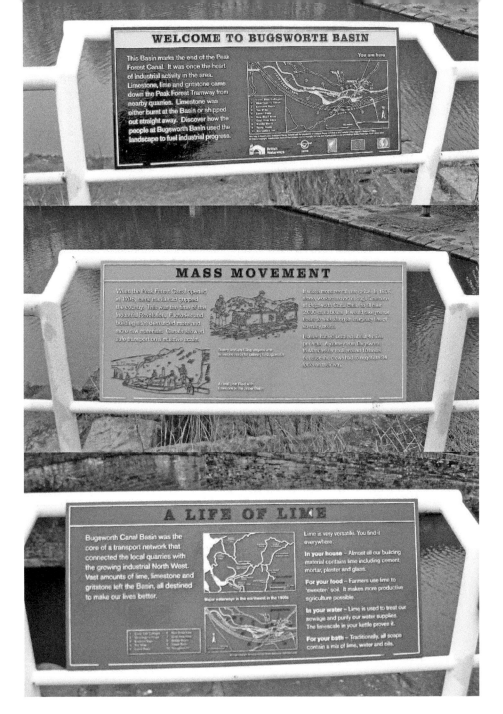

Bugsworth Basin

After remaining dry and derelict for many years, the canal basin at Bugsworth was restored by volunteers of the Inland Waterways Protection Society and was opened in March 2005. It is the only remaining canal/tramway interchange in the UK and an ancient monument protected by law. With funding in place, it is expected that a new visitor centre will be built here. The village is known as Buxworth and is twinned with Clayton in California which was founded by Jack Clayton, a one-time resident who emigrated to America in 1837.

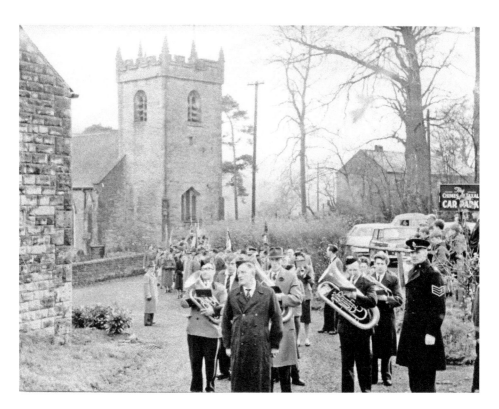

St James' church, Taxal

Remembrance Day, 1960, at St James' church, Taxal. The church is known as the Chimes of Taxal after the tower bells, the oldest dating from 1506. There were three bells in 1594, but by 1904 six bells rang the peal with two of the original plus four new ones. Some are inscribed with words from the Bible, and in 1987 £3,000 was raised to repair them. The tenor bell, which weighs 11cwt, was given by Samuel Evans, a former rector of the church. The car park sign has changed, the laurel bush to the left has grown and the dwelling to the far right has been extended.

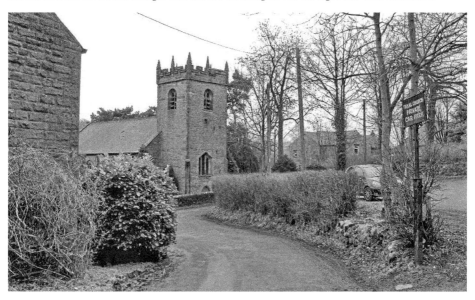

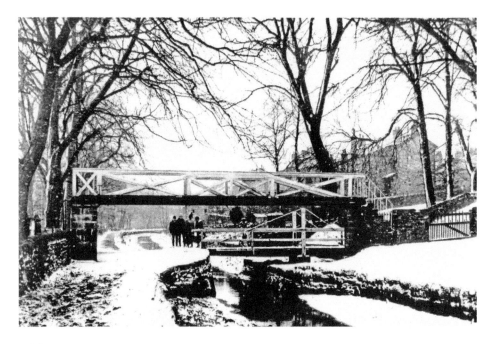

Bridge 34

The main structure of Bridge 34, on the Peak Forest Canal at Bridgemont, remains unchanged except for the metal handrails that replace the wooden ones. The canal had been drained for maintenance work in the winter of 1963. The swing bridge is no longer there so all pedestrians now have to climb the steps to access the towpath leading to the basin at Whaley Bridge. The Chapel Bypass, built over the canal, beyond the footbridge was first proposed in 1969. It carries A6 traffic around to the east, dividing the village of Bridgemont in half.

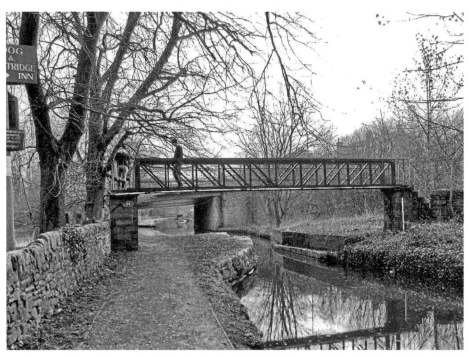

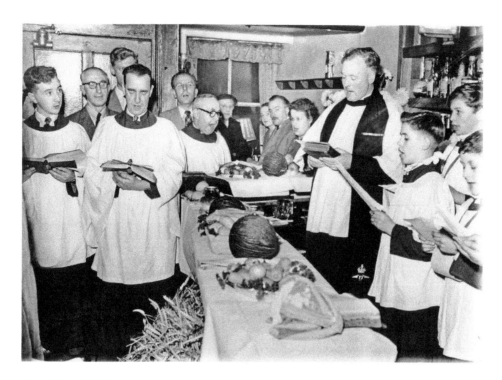

The Little Mill Inn

The Little Mill Inn, tucked away in the beautiful hamlet of Rowarth, dates from 1781 and was once a candlewick mill. The restored millwheel replaces one that was swept away by a flood in 1930. Today there is an outside seating area with play area for the children as well as the 'Derbyshire Belle' Pullman carriage, which came from the Brighton Belle Railway. In October 1956, The Reverend L.S. Weatherhead, along with the choir from St George's church, New Mills, conducted a harvest thanksgiving service inside the inn, with the local produce later used on the inn's menu.

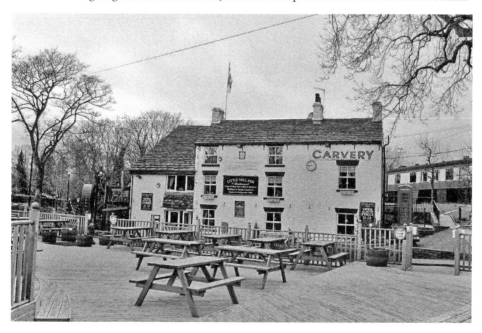

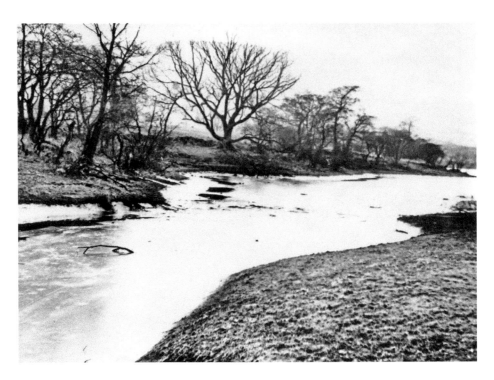

Coombs Reservoir

Combs is a delightful village beneath the slopes of Combs Moss between Whaley Bridge and Chapel-en-le-Frith in the Peak District. One of its more famous residents was Herbert Froode, one of the inventors of brake lining. The reservoir, which is next to a golf course, has changed very little over the years. There seems to be a variation in the spelling of the village name. The water authorities prefer Coombs whilst the sailing club prefers Combs. The Canal Company were not allowed to take water from the Tame, Goyt or Etherow rivers so Coombs and Toddbrook Reservoirs have acted as feeders for the Peak Forest Canal at Whaley.

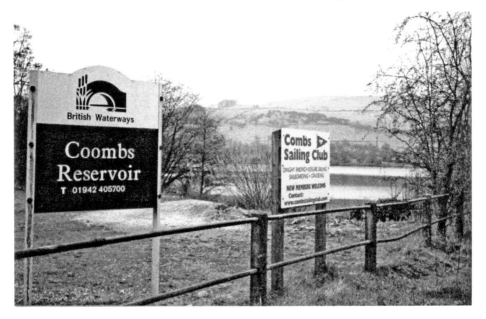

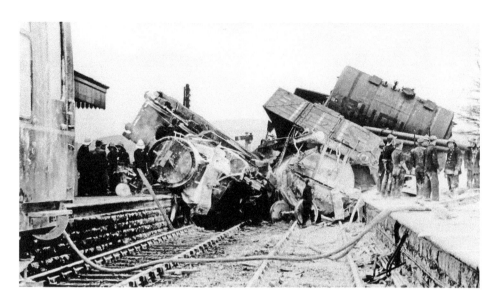

Chapel South Station

Chapel South Station was the scene of a rail disaster in February 1957. A runaway goods train from Dove Holes crashed into a diesel bound for Buxton at the Station in Chapel-en-le-Frith. Coal and lime were spilled over the track, the latter making the scene look as if snow had fallen. The old signal box on the right was destroyed but a glass station lamp remained intact. Today the scene is tranquil for passengers travelling from Manchester to Buxton, with a signal still visible in the centre and the Derbyshire hills beyond.

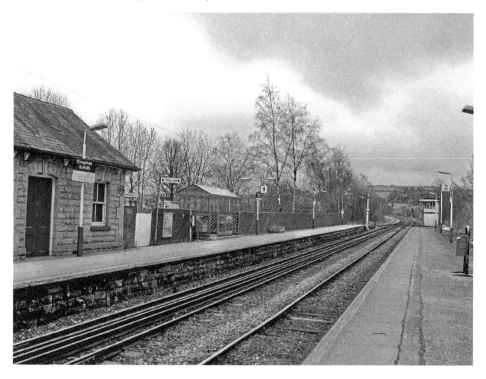

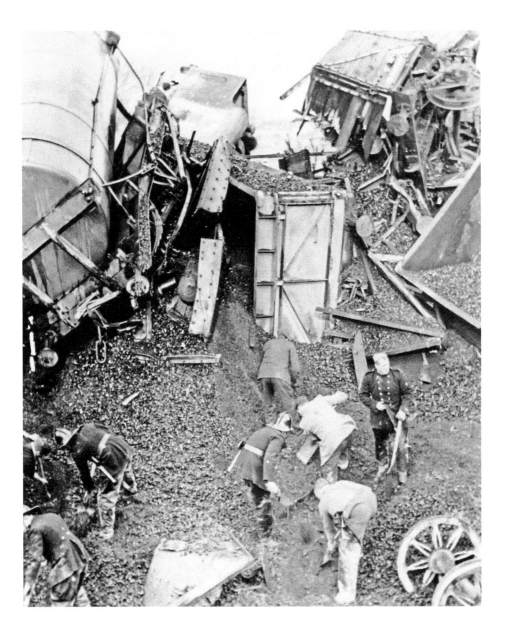

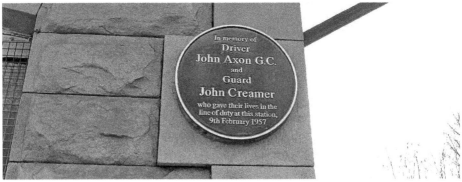

In memory of
Driver
John Axon G.C.
and
Guard
John Creamer
who gave their lives in the
line of duty at this station,
9th February 1957

Market Square

This page:

Chapel was founded in 1225 by foresters who were given permission by the Earl of Derby to build a chapel in the forest (a Chapel-en-le-Frith). In the cobbled Market Square, the medieval market cross still holds a commanding view of the High Street. Some changes have included the addition of street lighting, flower troughs on the railings, the lowering of some chimney pots, and the renovation of the building next to the Royal Oak. With the increase of traffic, vehicles now struggle to park and to pass each other in the streets.

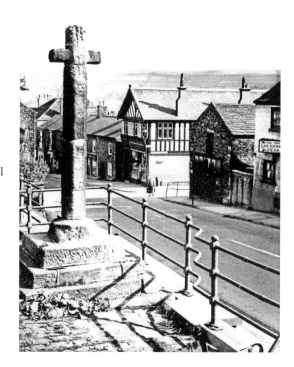

Railway Disaster, 1957

Opposite page:

Amongst the upturned wagons, firemen searched for the missing guard, John Creamer. The driver, John Axon, had already been found. Later, the driver was awarded the George Cross posthumously for his efforts in trying to prevent the crash. A Blue Plaque in memory of the two men from Stockport who were so tragically killed can be found on the station buildings. The driver's actor grandson was named after him; he had played the hospital boss in the TV series *The Royal* as well as parts in *Shameless*, *Phoenix Nights* and *Life on Mars*.

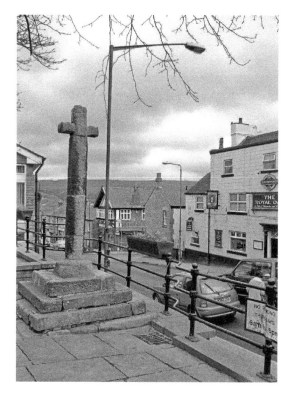

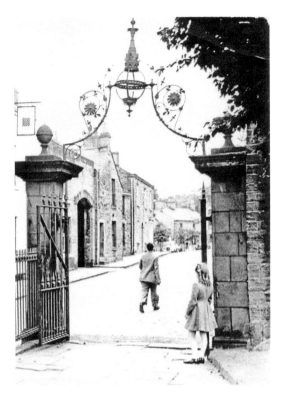

Chapel-en-le-Frith's parish church

Chapel-en-le-Frith's parish church is dedicated to St Thomas Becket, the English saint who became archbishop of Canterbury in 1162 and who was assassinated for his strong religious views in 1170. The church dates from 1225 and stands on a ridge overlooking the Upper Blackbrook valley. In 1954, the author of this book stood at the church gates looking down a virtually car-free street. At that time, an ornate arch supported the gas lamp over the entrance to the churchyard. In 2009, the church received a £300 grant from Derbyshire County Council to help with the substantial costs of maintaining the grounds.

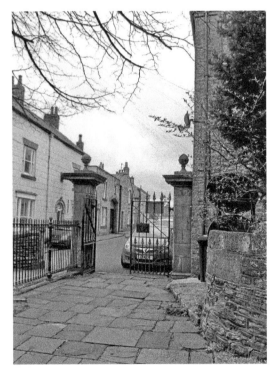

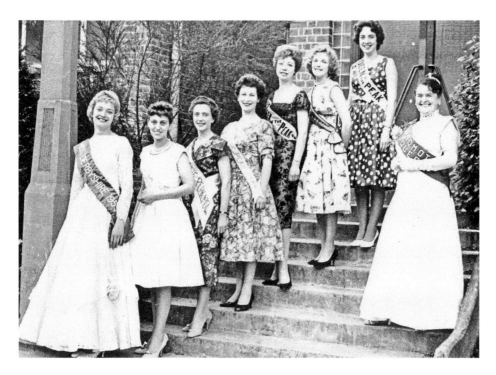

Ferodo at Chapel-en-le-Frith

Herbert Froode, a boot salesman from the village of Combs, made his name by developing woven cotton brakes for horse drawn wagons in the 1890s after observing carters tying old boots to the wooden brake blocks on their carts to provide more effective and longer lasting braking systems. He took over a mill in Chapel in 1897 and started to manufacture brake shoes. Many social events in the High Peak calendar have taken place in the old canteen at Ferodo. A factory queen was chosen annually, and in May 1960 various queens were chosen.

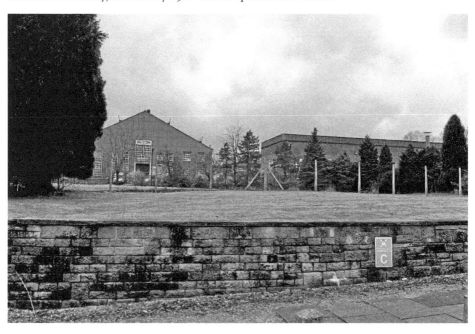

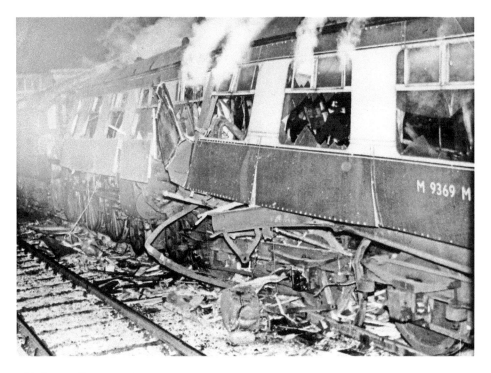

Chinley Railway Station

In March 1958, an express steam train from Luton crashed into the back of a slower train on platform 3 at Chinley Railway Station. Firemen can be seen inspecting the carriages with smoke emerging from the windows. Even though the engine toppled onto its side and a considerable amount of damage was done to the carriages, no one was killed on this Manchester City football supporters' special. The station was once an important junction for the Manchester to London line, with trains from Sheffield joining from the east.

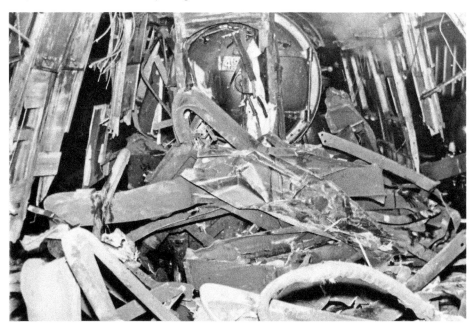

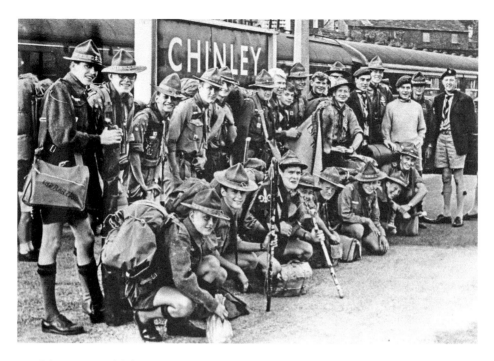

Danish Scouts, Chinley

The station once had a waiting room on each of the five platforms as well as a bookstall and refreshment room. Today the two railway tracks at Chinley station share the same platform. Trains come from Manchester and Sheffield via Edale and the Hope valley. In July 1965, twenty-two Danish scouts were met at the station to stay with the families of Chapel & Chinley Scouts. They had met local scouts at a Jamboree two years before. Whilst staying in Derbyshire they attended the World Jamboree at Chatsworth, home of the Duke and Duchess of Devonshire.

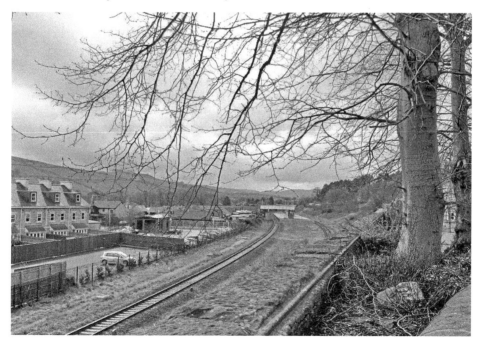

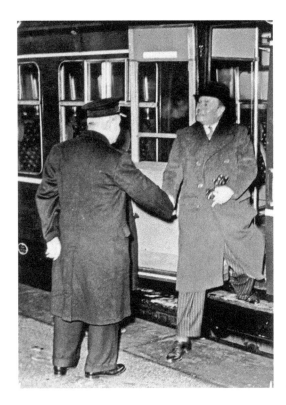

Chinley Station

In January 1956, Mr Pritchard, the stationmaster at Chinley, welcomed High Peak's MP, Mr Hugh Molsen, who at the time was the parliamentary secretary to the minister of transport. The MP arrived from Derby on a new light multiple diesel train. He had inspected the railway works at Derby on his way home from London. Today the railway serves workers and shoppers living in the villages nearby.

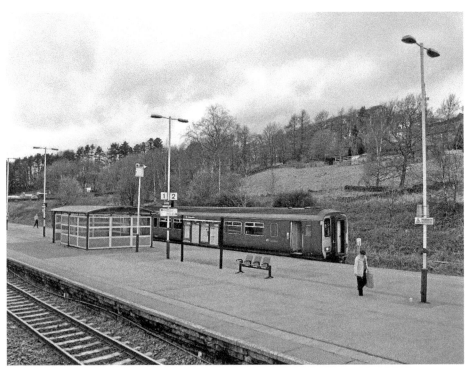

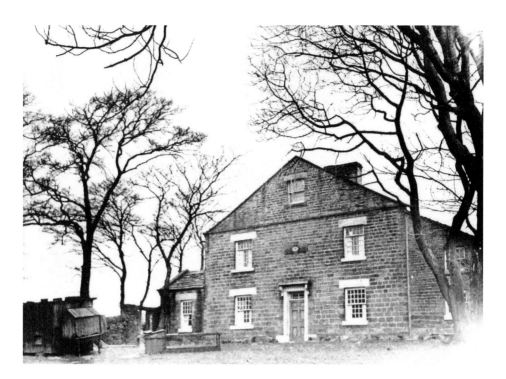

Peep-o-Day Farm

Peep-o-Day Farm at Chinley Head, just off the Hayfield to Chapel Road, was also called 'Hill's House.' It dates from 1841 and bears the inscription James & Mary Goddard. It has commanding views of South Head and Chinley Churn, hills that are popular with walkers. The name of the farm refers to the 'eye' above the front door, which contains a small window to catch the first early morning rays of the sun. The building is now a private dwelling and has been tastefully modernised with the addition of a front porch.

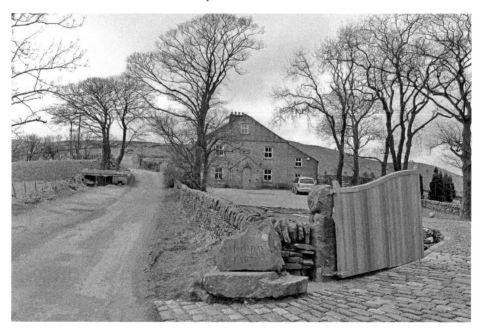

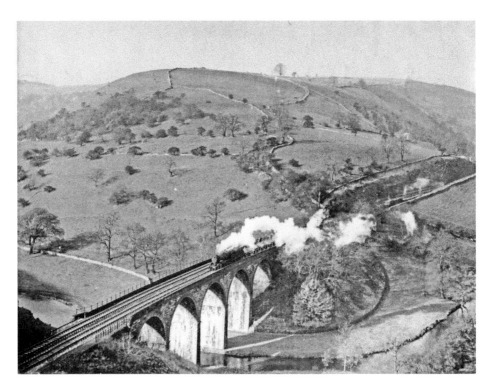

Monsal Viaduct

The Midland Railway ran through the Peak District over the 80ft high Monsal Viaduct from 1867. The Richard Beeching report 'Reshaping British Railways' closed the line in 1968. The 8 mile Monsal Trail from Bakewell, used by walkers and cyclists, ends at Blackwell Mill, but a train still uses the quarry route into Buxton to transport limestone. Several rail tunnels were built through the hills and the line crosses the River Wye six times. Cotton mills at Cressbrook and Litton brought industry to the valley.

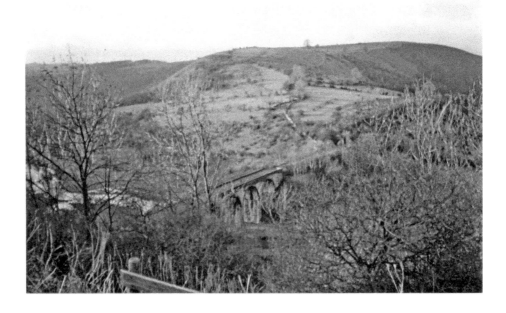

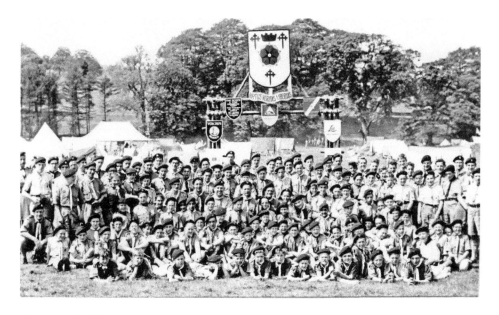

Chatsworth House

A jamboree was held at Chatsworth House in June 1960 where 2,800 Scouts and 1,800 Guides attended from all parts of the world. The Chief Scout, at that time, was Sir Charles MacLean and Cub Scout Trevor Howard from Glossop, took the 'Grand Howl'. Under the Glossop coat of arms, some of the town's factories, Volcrepe, Isaac Jackson, Lux Lux, Levi Jackson and Flexi Brushes were advertised. The motto *Virtus Veritas Liberta* means 'for moral perfection, truth & freedom'. The large park, laid out by Capability Brown, makes Chatsworth the ideal place to host so many different outdoor events.

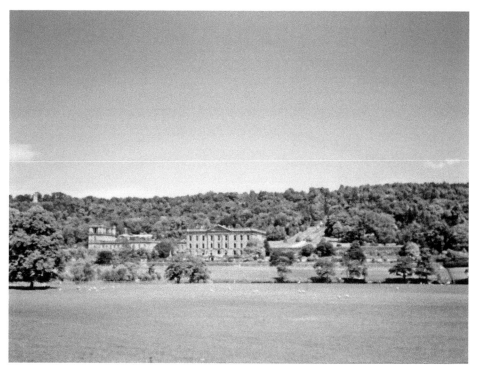

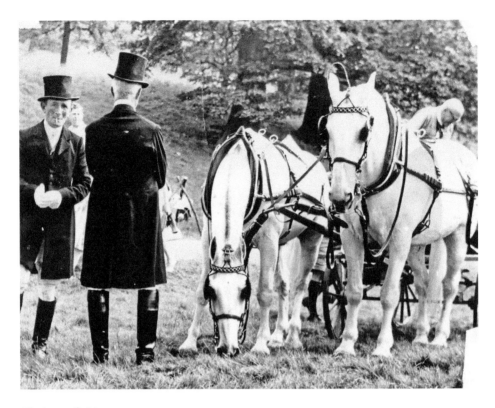

Chatsworth House

Bess of Hardwick had Chatsworth House built in the reign of Elizabeth I, when she married into the Cavendish family. Her marriage to William Cavendish was her second marriage but the 1st Duke of Devonshire had this house taken down. The present house, beside the River Derwent, dates from 1550 with the exterior being late seventeenth century. The 11th Duke of Devonshire, Andrew Cavendish, was mayor of Buxton from 1952-54 and died in 2004 aged eighty-four. At the Scout Jamboree in 1960, the Duke's carriage drivers were taking a break from their duties.

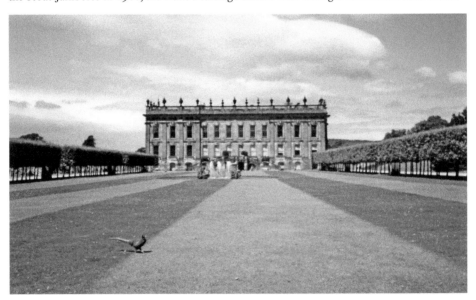

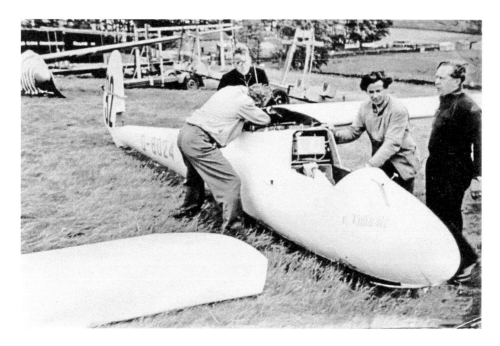

Gliding at Great Hucklow

Gliding off Campbell Edge at Hucklow in July 1954. Gliding at Hucklow has drawn enthusiasts and spectators over the decades. Along with many other Derbyshire villages, a well is dressed each year. Pictures consisting of flower petals and seed heads represent both traditional and modern themes. This one celebrated Elizabeth II's Golden Jubilee. The custom reputed to have started in Celtic times was revived in 1349 in Tissington. It began as a thanksgiving to God for the continued supply of water, and even in times of drought most wells have never dried up.

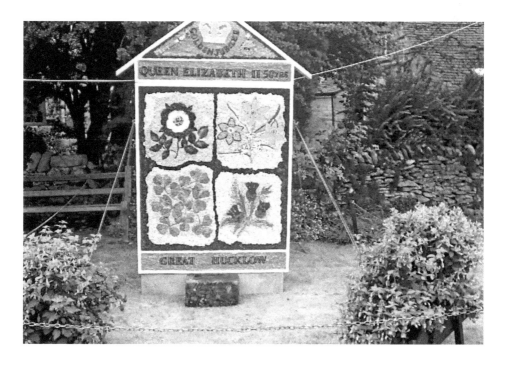

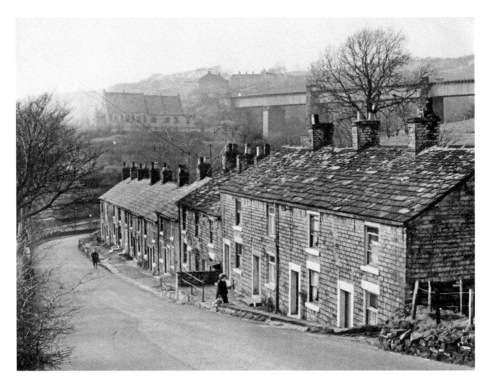

Long Lane, Charlesworth

These cottages on Long Lane, Charlesworth, were nicknamed New York after three families living in them emigrated to America to find work and escape unemployment caused by the cotton famine. In 1960, a lorry with a 15-ton load ran backwards down the lane crashing into the end cottage. The houses were eventually demolished in 1961 and the space now provides parking for the Roman Catholic Immaculate Conception church. The village of Broadbotton is in the distance.

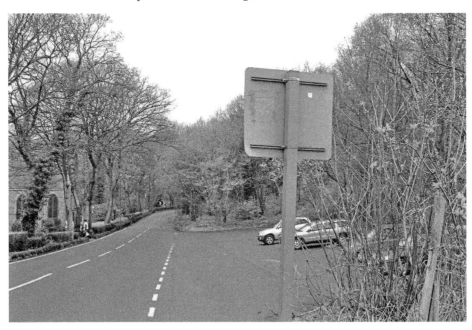

Besthill Bridge on the Chesire/ Derbyshire Border

The River Etherow marks the divide between two counties at this point, on one side is the village of Broadbottom in Cheshire and on the other is Charlesworth in Derbyshire. The railway viaduct is a Grade II listed structure that stands 138ft high and 555ft long. It was opened in 1842, and the stone pillars are original but the brick pillars replaced some timber ones in 1859. The overhead electrics are no longer required as diesel trains from Glossop to Manchester now cross the bridge. Underneath the viaduct the narrow Besthill road bridge operates a one-way system to convey traffic.

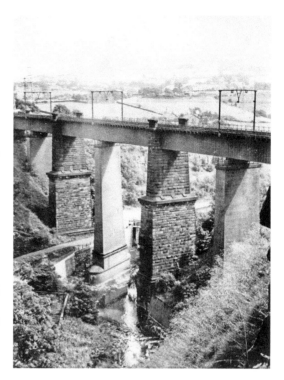

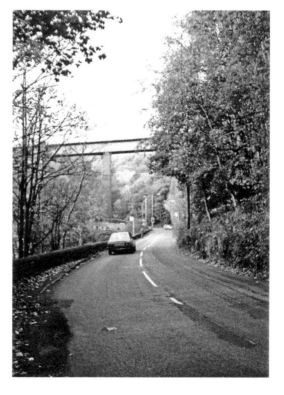

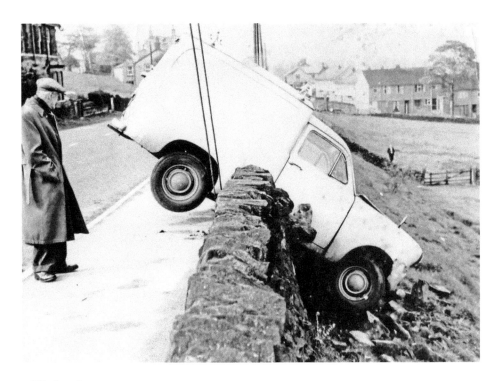

Mills Road

The new patches of wall on the Hayfield to new Mills Road indicate that vehicles still ignore the speed limit. After this incident in May 1961, the driver of the Standard Van was unhurt and caught the bus home. To the right of the houses, more dwellings have been built and the top field has become a sports ground. The rivers Sett and Goyt flow through New Mills in a gorge called the Torrs which has a magnificent Millennium Walkway over the waters. Love Hearts and Refreshers have been made in the town from 1940 when sweet manufacturers Swizzels Matlow Ltd. established their factory on Union Road.

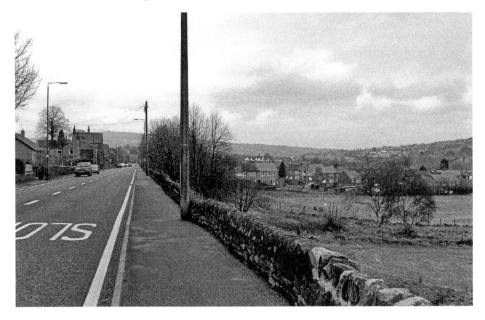

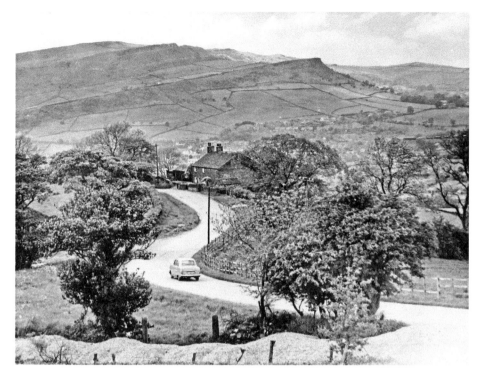

Whitehough

The road from Chinley to Chapel goes through Whitehough. This view, taken from near Hall Farm, shows the village of Chinley and the beautiful Derbyshire scenery including Cracken Edge. Although at first sight there seems to be little change to the scene, with goods wagons pulled by a steam train travelling towards the station, to the right of the cottage more housing has been built in Chinley and the Chapel Bypass now cuts across the valley.

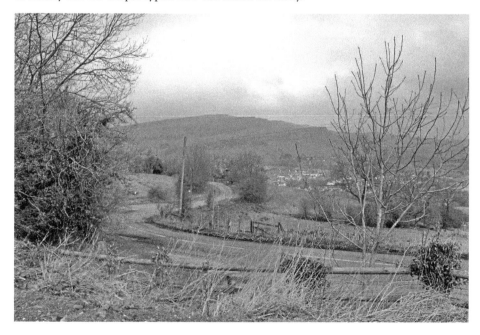

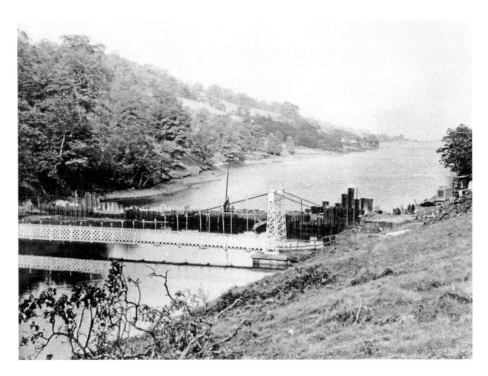

The Goyt Valley

The Goyt Valley in the Peak District National Park was formed by the movement of rocks millions of years ago. In 1909, three men were killed in the valley at the Chilworth Gun Powder factory. The river, meadowlands and hamlet of Goytsbridge were flooded to create the Fernilee and Errwood Reservoirs. The dam was completed after four years of construction work and officially opened by the Duchess of Kent in 1968. The old ornate bridge was demolished when the new Derbyshire Bridge was complete. A Roman road, known as The Street, runs through the valley next to the car park to Pym Chair. The Errwood Sailing Club now makes use of the water here.

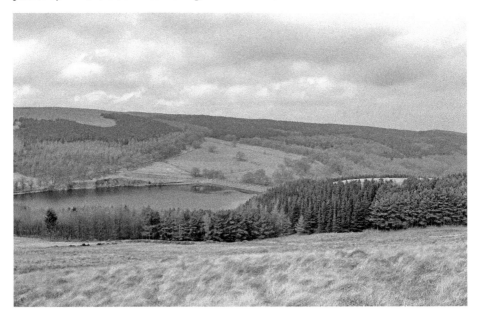

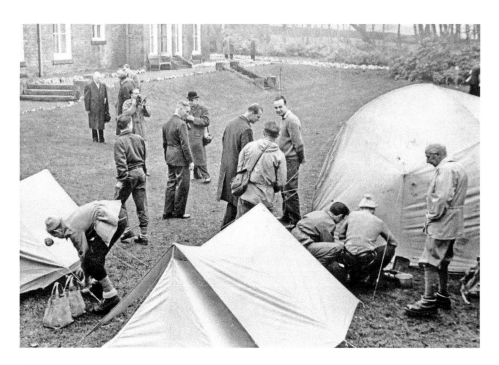

Whitehall Centre

Just off Long Hill – the road from Whaley Bridge to Buxton – is the Whitehall Centre. It was the first outdoor education centre in the country. Sir Jack Longland, who also opened the Lea Green Sports Centre near Matlock, founded it in 1951. In November 1958, as part of a royal tour of the High Peak area, the Duke of Edinburgh visited the centre. Since that time, a conservatory has been added to the hall and is used as the dining room. Prince Philip also went to see the climbing course at Castle Naze near Chapel and to Ferodo, the brake lining factory.

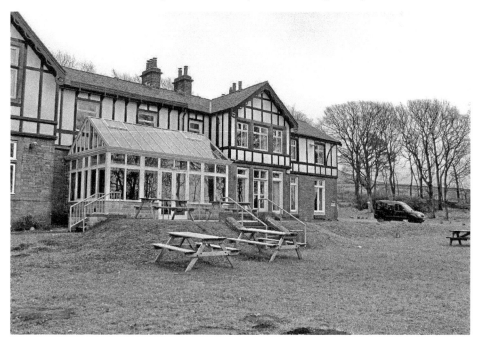

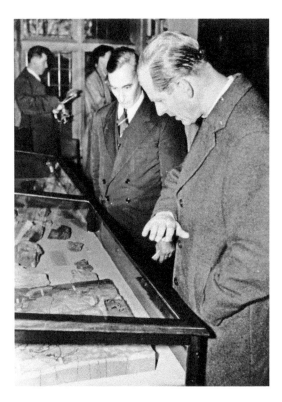

Whitehall

Inside Whitehall, Prince Philip was shown a display of local archaeological finds (now housed in Buxton Museum) by Sir Jack Longland (1905-1993). He was knighted in 1948 and was an outstanding sportsman, radio broadcaster and a member of the team that attempted Everest in 1933. On the wall behind Mr Bob Higginbotham, the resident chef, there is a plaque commemorating the time that the senior department of Elizabeth College Guernsey spent the years of the Exile, 1940-45, at Whitehall. Many of the girls and their families have since visited to recall their time at Whitehall.

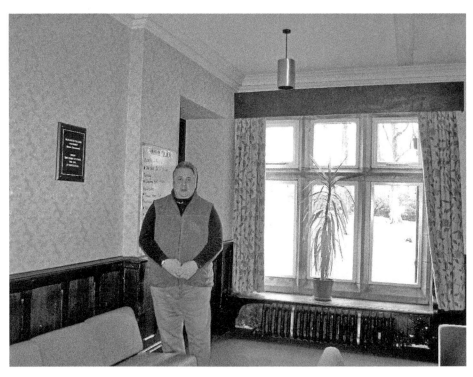

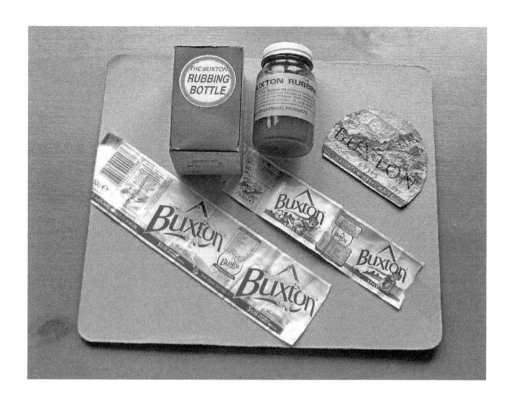

Buxton

Buxton has been a popular spa town since the Romans established thermal baths there and called the town *Aquae Arnemetiae*, meaning 'The Spa of the Goddess of the Grove'. St Anne's Well was presented to Buxton in 1940. It still flows freely with spring water and people regularly queue to fill their containers in the town centre. The swimming pool is also filled with the 28 degree thermal waters and in the Pump Room and Cavendish Arcades there is evidence of where people 'took to the waters'. Nestle Waters UK Ltd. also bottles the natural mineral water in the town. Although produced in Staffordshire, Buxton Rub was widely sold as a relief for pain.

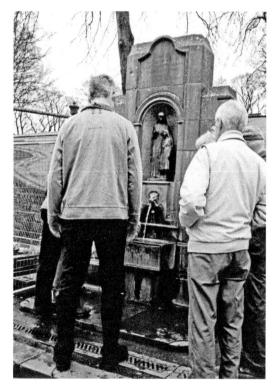

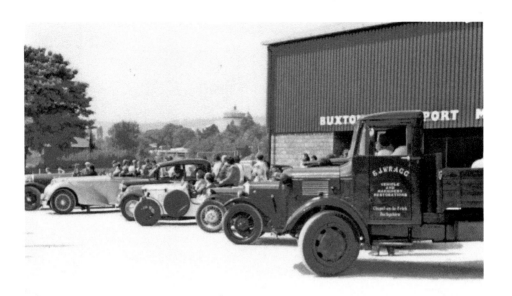

Buxton Transport Museum

Vintage car enthusiast Peter Clark founded the Buxton Transport Museum, which was opened in 1980 by television presenter Stuart Hall. It closed after only three years and occupied part of the land where the Buxton Mineral Water Company now stands near to the Railway Station. At the G20 Summit in 2009, American President Barack Obama was seen drinking Buxton spring water. The water flows naturally to the surface, untouched and pure, from a depth of 1,500 metres, having filtered for 5,000 years through the ancient limestone of the Peak District.

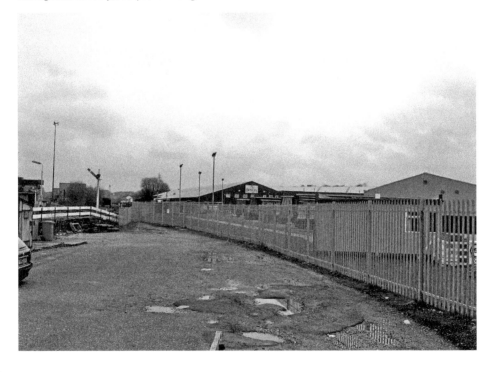

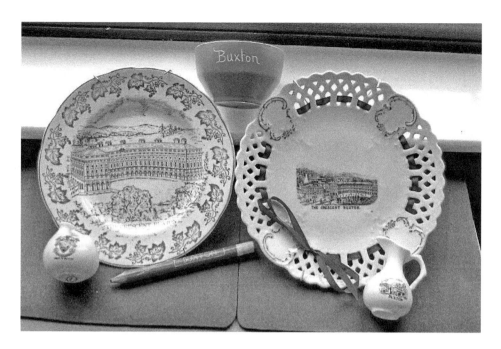

Buxton Crescent

Visitors to Buxton have always been able to buy souvenirs of their stay. Blue pottery with a white rim bearing the town's name was very popular in the mid-1900s, especially if your surname was Buxton! Ribbon plates with pictures of the Crescent and trinkets, bearing the town's coat of arms have all graced the homes of visitors. The Crescent, designed by John Carr of York, was built between 1780 and 1789 for the 5th Duke of Devonshire and is Grade I listed. Major refurbishment is planned to create a seventy-nine-bedroom, five-star spa hotel. Specialist retail units, a visitor and tourist centre and a tearoom are planned for the Pump Room.

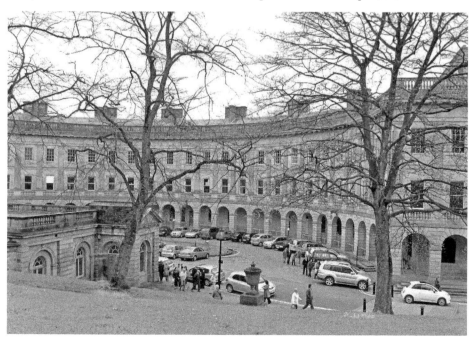

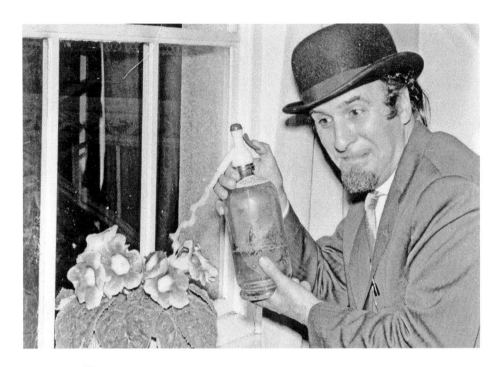

Buxton Pavilion

Buxton hosts many events and festivals at the Opera House and in the award winning Pavilion Gardens. The River Wye flows through the 23 acres of beautiful parkland with attractions for all ages. In August 1962, Bernard Stanley Bilk – better known as Mr Acker Bilk, MBE – the clarinettist was asked to switch on the illuminations in the Pavilion Gardens. Later he pretended to use the town's spa water from a soda siphon to water one of the plants from the conservatory, which is always a spectacle of colour. He became famous for the song *Stranger on the Shore* that stayed in the charts for fifty-five weeks. The pavilion is also a venue for civil weddings and banquets.

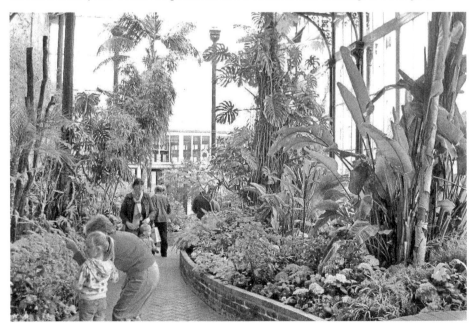

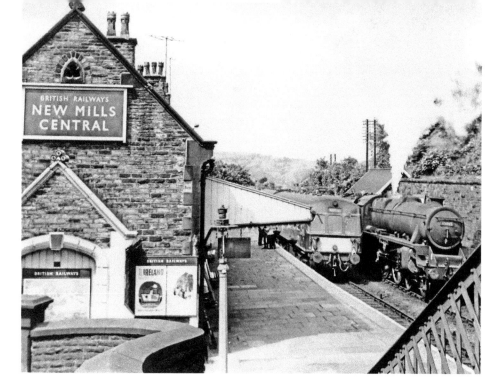

New Mills

New Mills was formed from the hamlets of Beard, Ollersett, Thornsett and Whitle; it has two railway stations, Newtown and Central. Both steam and diesel engines were running in the earlier photograph and trips to Ireland were advertised on the billboards at Central Station. Today the station seems to have changed little, but gone is the British Rail maroon paint and the gas lamps that illuminated the platforms which have since been resurfaced. The metal structure of the booking office canopy is exposed and the smoke from the steam trains no longer blackens the stone buildings. The wooden side door has gone, as has the roof of the waiting area on the right hand platform.

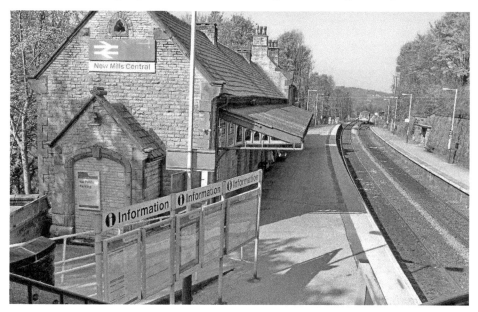

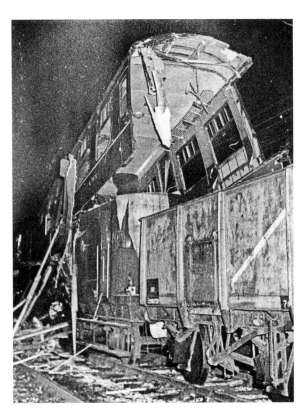

New Mills Train Crash, 1960

In October 1960, New Mills was the scene of a train crash when a six-coach diesel train ploughed into the back of a goods train. The driver, Mr E.S. Jones, and two children, Philip Wheatcroft and Margaret Hibbert, were injured. Diesel/electric trains now travel on the lines. From New Mills, Newtown Station passengers can travel to Buxton or Manchester and from New Mills, Central Station, there are journeys to Sheffield and Manchester on the Hope Valley service.

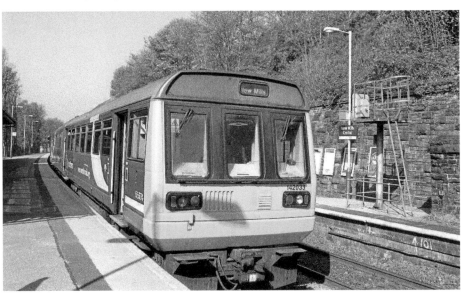

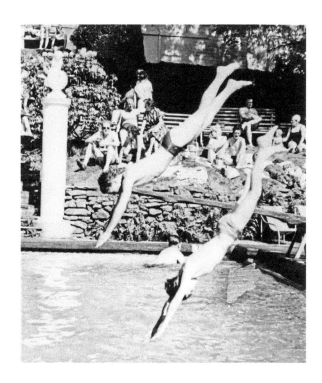

Park Hall

The place for the whole family to go in the summer of 1963 was Park Hall, off the Glossop to Hayfield Road, at Little Hayfield. The outdoor pool was well used by locals as well as those who came from surrounding areas and those who came in double-decker buses from Manchester. A gate bearing the sign 'Park Hall Pool' in front of the pools remains and is the only evidence of its existence. Above is the 1,224ft high Lantern Pike, which was purchased by public subscription in 1950 as a memorial to Edwin Royce who fought for the freedom to roam the hills. The hill got its name from warning beacons that used to be lit here. The countryside is now managed by The National Trust.

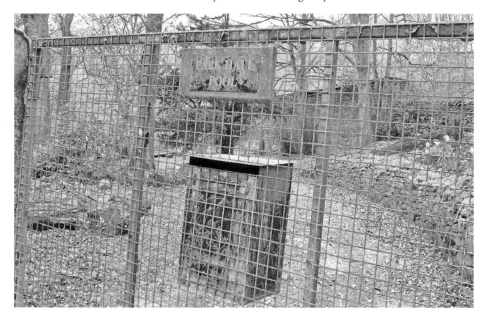

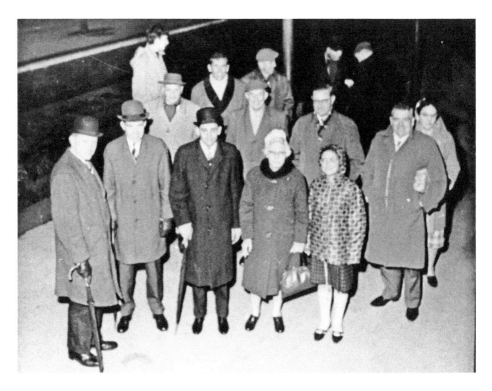

Hayfield Railway Station

Hayfield Railway Station closed in 1970 and some of the last passengers were waiting on the platform for the last train to Manchester. The line was opened in 1868 and goods wagons brought raw materials and coal to the mills in the Sett Valley. Today the information centre and bus station mark the spot where the trains once stopped. British Rail sold the Hayfield to New Mills line to Derbyshire County Council in 1973 and after reclamation work the Sett Valley Trail was opened in September 1979. The 2½ mile route now provides a delightful trail for walkers, cyclist and horse riders.

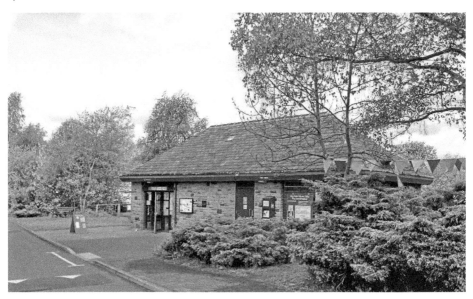

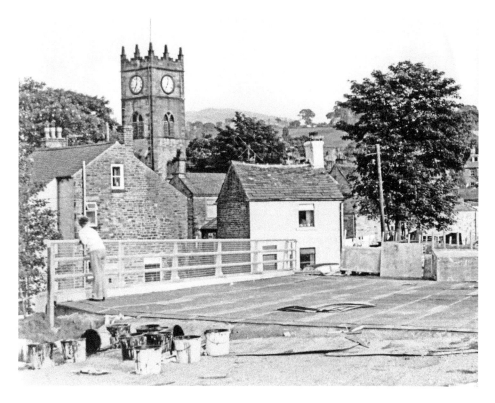

Hayfield Village

The village of Hayfield is listed as 'Hedfeld' in the Domesday Book of 1086 when it was part of Glossop. The village was bypassed in 1978 when a new road was built to link with the A624 Glossop Road. It necessitated the building of a road-bridge over the river and access from the bus station to the village is via a pedestrian crossing or subway. Horse riders using the Pennine Bridleway, can also cross the busy road with the aid of a special wide crossing with controls at their height.

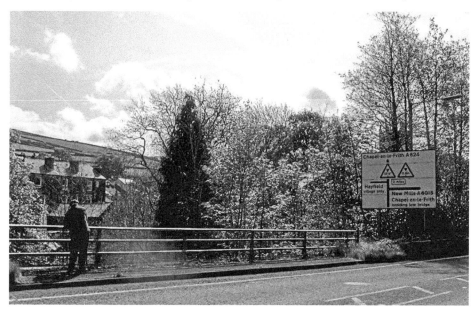

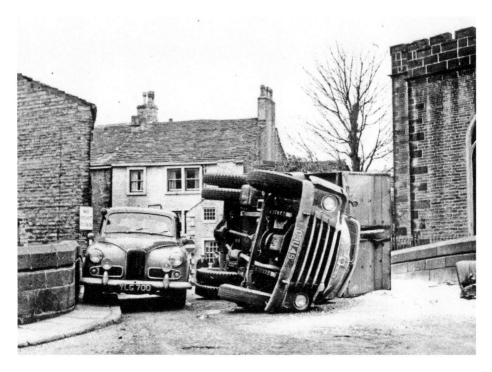

Hayfield Centre

Before the bypass was built, all traffic travelling towards Glossop had to drive through the village. In February 1961, a runaway lorry overturned as it negotiated the narrow bridge in the centre of Hayfield. The driver and his seat were thrown out and the contents of his load were spilt over the road whilst other vehicles were still squeezing past the scene. The Bull's Head is the white building behind and St Matthew's church, dating from 1818, is to the side.

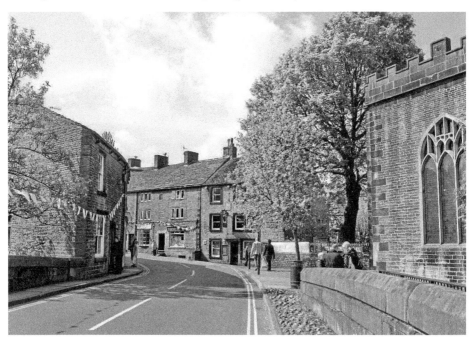

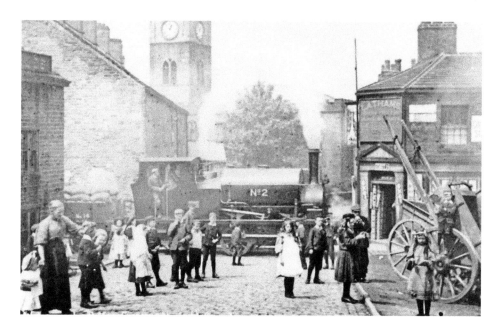

Kinder Printworks

The site of the Kinder Printworks, which was demolished in 1900, was used for the Kinder Reservoir. Trains used to cross Church Street, Hayfield, with materials for its construction. The first locomotives on the line were 0-6-0 and 4-4-2 Tank Engines. Stockport Corporation owned locomotive No. 2 from 1908-1910. After completion of the reservoir in July 1912, trains ceased to travel on this stretch. Latham's store to the right, which was advertising Oxo and Colman's Mustard, is still a village store. To the left are the George Hotel, The Village Chippy, the Bull's Head and St Matthew's church.

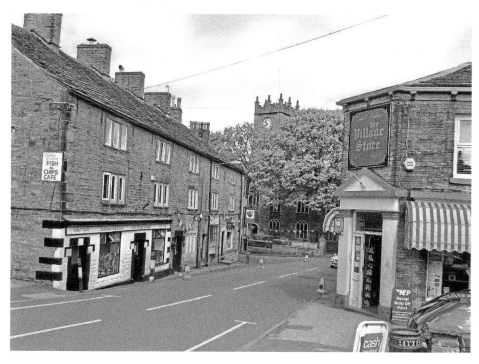

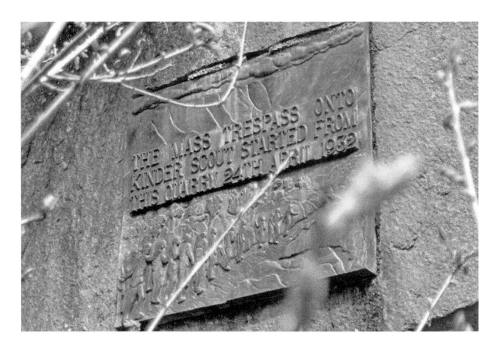

Mass Trespass, 1932

On 24 April 1932, five ramblers were sentenced to prison after minor scuffles with the Duke of Devonshire's gamekeeper, William Clough. Ramblers, led by Benny Rothman, had rallied at the disused Bowden Bridge Quarry before setting off on the Mass Trespass of Kinder Scout to assert their right to roam on Britain's open land. A plaque commemorating this historical event was unveiled at New Mills Town Hall in 1984 by eighty-two-year-old Benny himself. In the quarry car park at Hayfield, another plaque and a carved bench also commemorate the event that was instrumental in the start of national parks. The Peak District National Park was the first to be created in 1951.

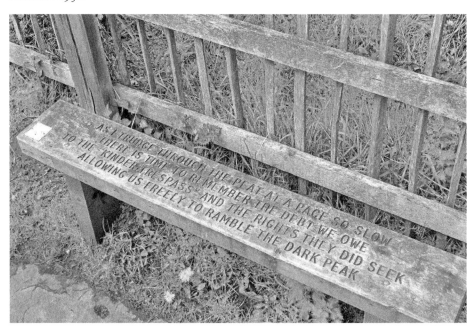

Kinder Scout

Kinder Scout is one of the toughest walks because ramblers can experience atrocious weather conditions, yet the lower paths leading to it are some of the most beautiful. The delightful walk from Hayfield by the Rivers Sett and Kinder passes the former site of Kinder Printworks, now occupied by the Camping and Caravanning Club and this packhorse bridge near Oak Bank. Several gates and bridges mark the field boundaries to Kinder. In 1966, the widow of a rambler opened a footbridge in his memory. A new footbridge, in the same style, was recently carved from a sweet chestnut tree that had grown on the Grindsbrook valley of Kinder.

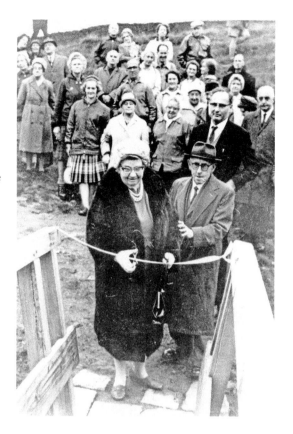

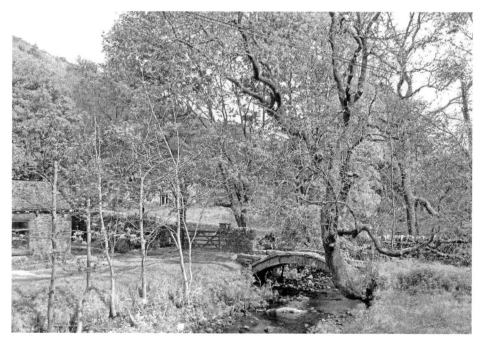

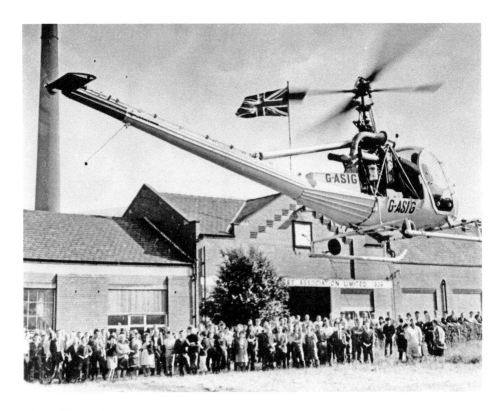

The Calico Trail

From the 1700s, the clear running waters of the River Sett and the streams that fed it made ideal conditions for spinning using water powered equipment. Hayfield also had papermaking mills, calico printing and dye factories. Woods Printworks was built in the late eighteenth century and had various uses up to 1969. Its chimney came down in 1972 and it was finally demolished to make way for new housing in 1990. Today, a guided walk called the Calico Trail starts at the signpost to the right. In the 1960s, Sir William Lees flew into Hayfield on his visit to the Calico Printers Association works.

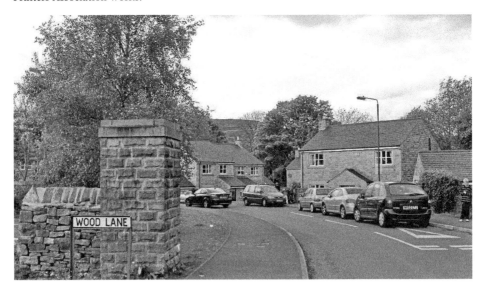

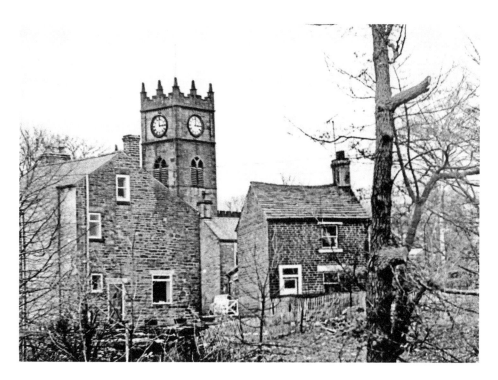

Hayfield May Queen Festival

Hayfield has had a May Queen Festival on the second Saturday in the month since 1928. In 2009 the theme was the sea, and houses, pubs and shops all joined in to celebrate. The carnival procession moved through the village to the delight of the large crowds. Characters from *Star Wars* passed the memorial gardens in front of the Bears Pits off Market Street, which was once a place where bear baiting took place. The view of the church is now somewhat obscured, compared to the photograph taken in the 1960s.

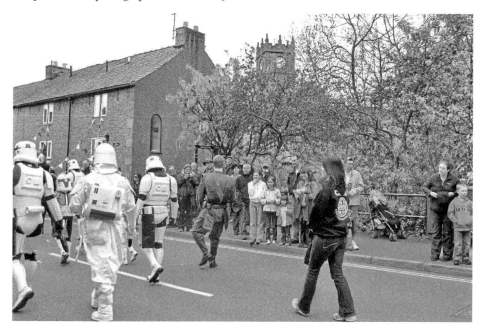

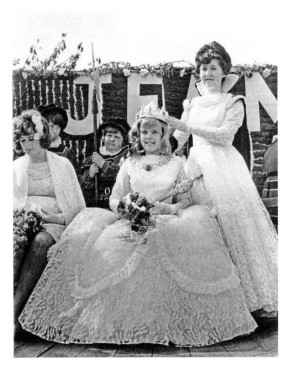

Derbyshire Queens

In 1966, Jean Harrison was crowned May Queen by the retiring queen. Many Rose Queens from the surrounding villages, as well as queens representing various charities, gather to join in the festival celebrations. The Queen of the Peak is chosen from the queens who represent each village in Derbyshire's High Peak. Rachel Saxby had been selected at Chapel-en-le-Frith's Methodist chapel to represent the Peak for 2009. Many years ago, this event took place in the canteen at the Ferodo works.

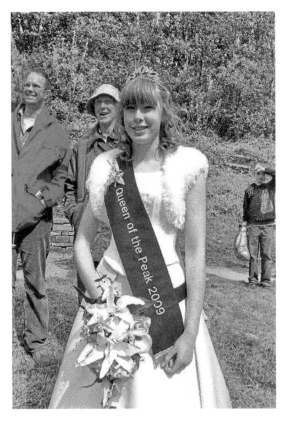

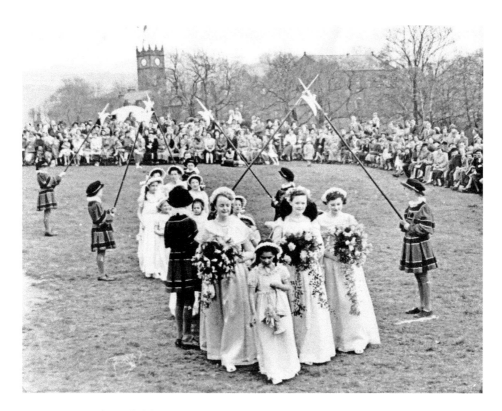

May Queen of Hayfield

In 1951, May Queen Patricia walked through the Beefeater guard of honour on the Old School Field in Hayfield. In 2009, the tradition still takes place; Annie Hallam was May Queen, Anouska Manion was Princess and Holly Howard was the Rosebud. Onlookers, local dignitaries and the 'royalty' are entertained by dancers and various display teams whilst stalls and the fairground entertain others attending. In the village, bands, morris dancers, the pubs, shops, church and the village cricket team all provide sustenance or entertainment.

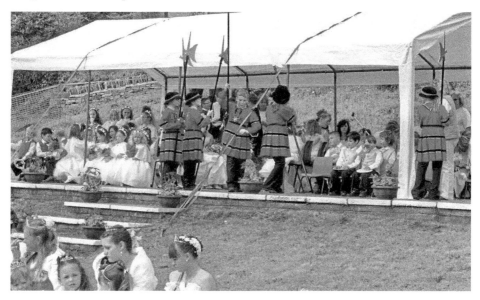

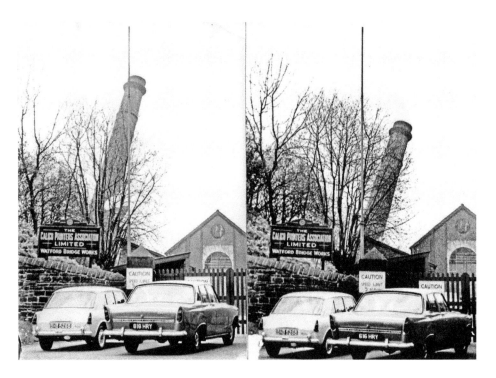

Watford Bridge Works

Watford Bridge Works used to be known as London Place and began in 1801 by Bridge and Hart. It stands just off the road through Birch Vale on the way to New Mills and it was a thriving concern in 1868 along with the Calico Printing works. Textiles ceased at Watford Bridge in 1929 and the mill chimney was demolished in the 1960s. The STP Group who produce joinery products, doors, stairs and windows now use the factory.

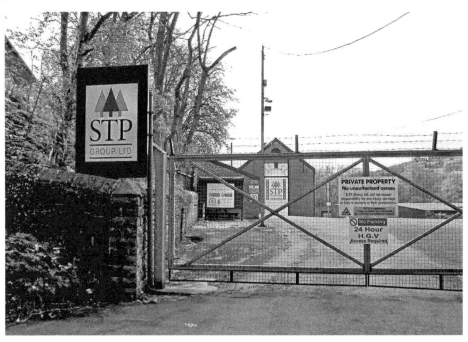

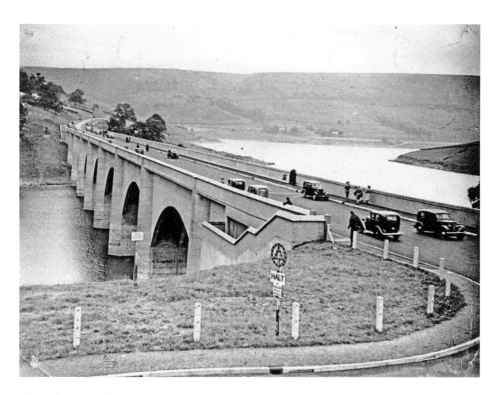

The Ashopton Viaduct

The Ashopton Viaduct links the A57 road from Sheffield to Glossop via the Snake Pass. The road was a turnpike road opened in 1821 to replace the old packhorse routes lead by jaggers. The Derwent and Howden dams had been constructed between 1901 and 1916. The Ladybower Reservoir was begun in May 1935 by the Derwent Valley Water Board to supply water to the residents of Sheffield, Derby, Nottingham and Leicester. After much opposition to its construction the reservoir was finally opened in 1945 by George VI, drawing large crowds to watch the event.

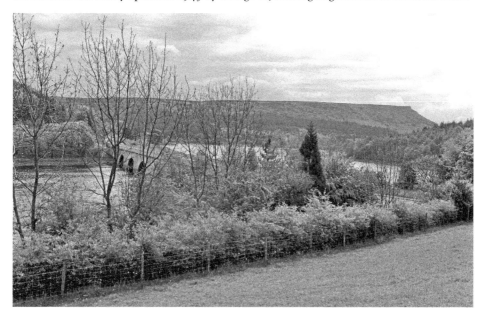

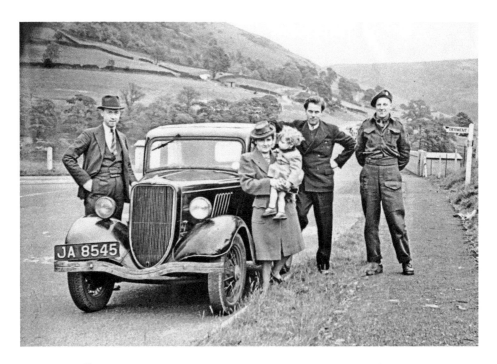

Derwent Valley

The 617 Dambuster's Squadron trained with bouncing bombs at Ladybower over the Derwent & Howden reservoirs in May 1943 prior to their raid on the Ruhr dam in Germany the same year. Many more visitors have been drawn to the Derwent Valley since the viaduct was built. In 1945, Harry & Janey Buxton, with their son from Hadfield, brought Canadian cousins Walter and Stanley Buxton to see the Derwent area and the ruins of Nether Ashop Farm and Underbank Farm where their ancestors had once lived. The scene has changed little except for new road signs and modern vehicles.

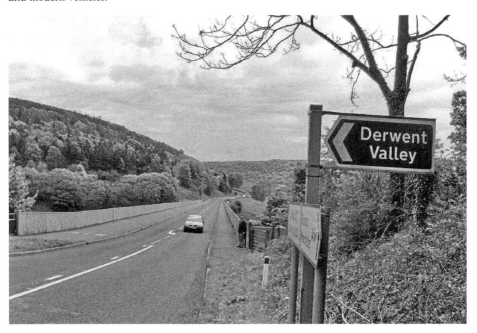

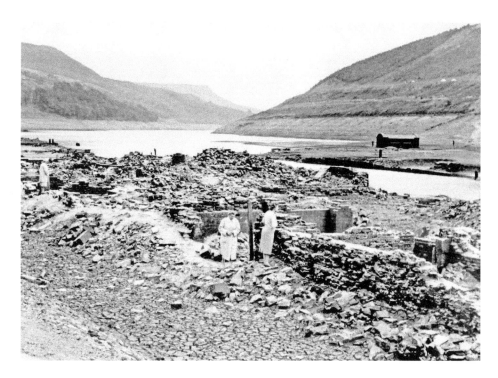

Ladybower Dam

The construction of Ladybower Dam caused the demise of Derwent and Ashopton in the 1940s; the remains of the villages were submerged leaving only the tower of St John's and St James' church protruding. In December 1947, the tower was blown up, and the ruins of Derwent Hall, dating from 1672, re-appeared in 1976 and 1989 when the water level was abnormally low. The building in the distance was a water valve house. The only structures to be saved were a seventeenth-century packhorse bridge, moved stone by stone to Slippery Stones at the top end of Howden Reservoir, and Ashes Farm, because of its high position on the hillside.

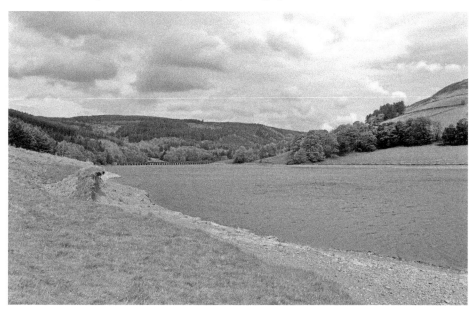

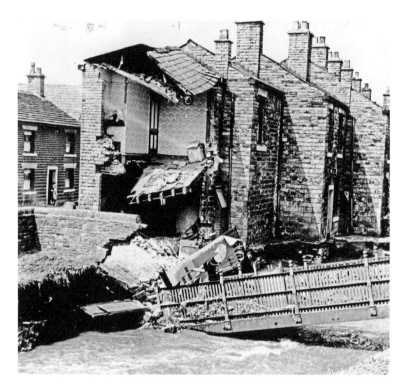

Glossop Brook

The swollen waters of Glossop Brook have caused severe flooding to local property and business premises many times. One of the worst floods was in 1944 when water swept through the town demolishing anything in its way and carrying logs from Turn Lee Paper Mill many miles down stream. The iron bridge off High Street West collapsed and swept away a lady from George Street, carrying her body down into the River Etherow. Today, after improvements to the flood defences, the water doesn't cause as much damage and pedestrians heading for the Tesco store use a bridge over Glossop Brook in safety.

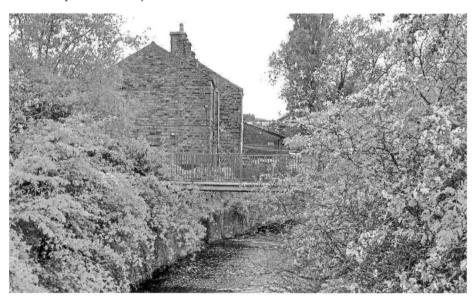

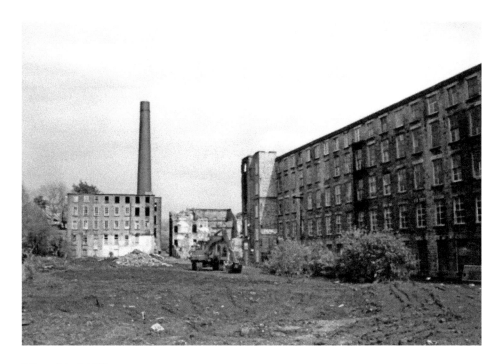

Wren Nest Mill

Wren Nest Mill, at the side of Glossop Brook, became known as Sumner's Mill from 1829 after the proprietor Francis Sumner. Using steam power for the weaving machines, there were 120,000 spindles and 2,700 looms by 1884, and it was the third largest mill in Glossop. After use by several other companies, the mill lay empty for many years. The chimney was demolished and a retail park was created. In about 2006, the building on the right was changed to apartments with business premises below.

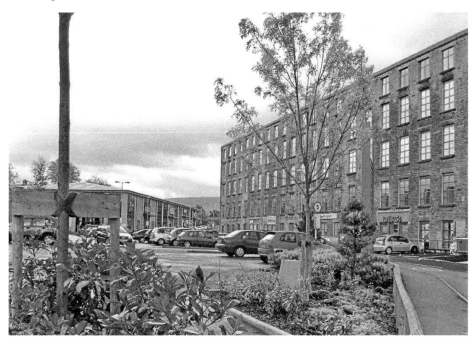

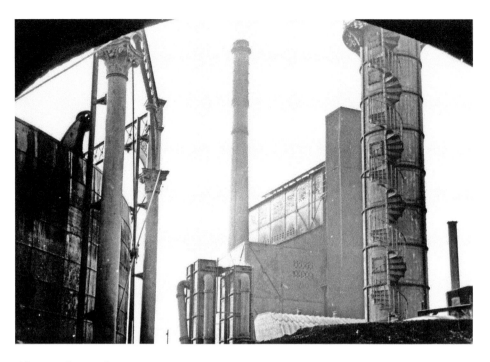

Glossop Gasworks

The gasworks on Arundel Street, Glossop, was set up by the Duke of Norfolk in 1845. It cost £6,000 and the money was raised from £10 shares. The shareholders were known as the Glossop Gas Light Company and dividends were paid up to nationalisation in 1949. In 1957, it was announced that the gasworks was to close and the site demolished. In 1995, the site became a Kwik Save store, later changing to an Aldi store, and the office building is used by Wains stationery business. Although the metal processing plant of Ferro-Alloy's on Surrey Street has closed, the 1980s chimney that once diffused chemical gasses remains.

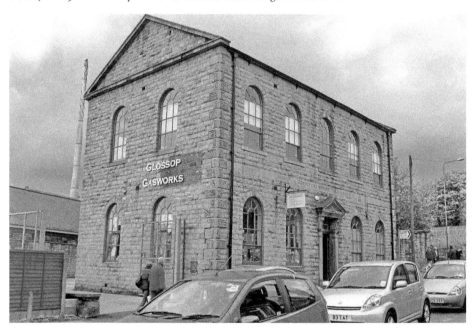

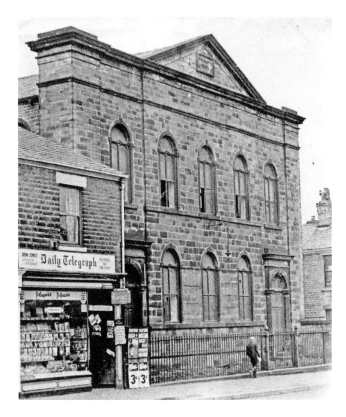

Glossop's Wesleyan Chapel

John Wesley founded Methodism in 1739 and Glossop's Wesleyan Chapel was named after him. It stood on the corner of the High Street and Chapel Street. It was demolished in April 1965 as part of the local Methodist reorganisation scheme after 125 years service in Glossop. The new chapel was built around the corner on Chapel Street in 1966. Don Jones' newsagent's shop is now closed, but at the time the *Daily Mail* was only 3d. On the site of the chapel retail units – currently the Ruchi restaurant and Super Pound – were built.

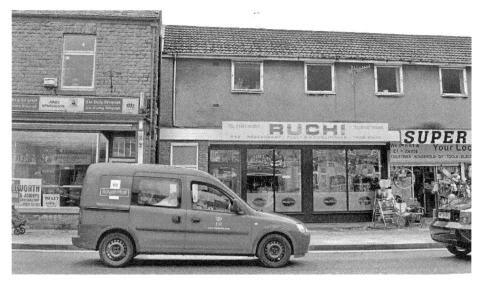

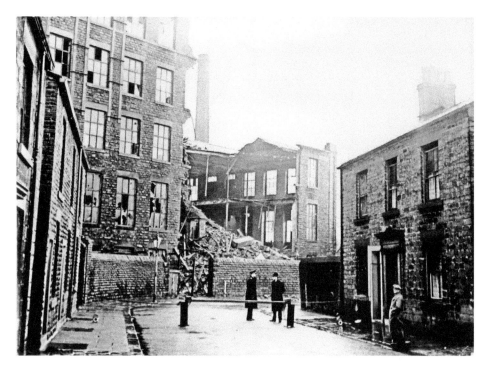

Shepley Mill

Shepley Mill, on Chapel Street, was used for cotton spinning and was built in 1810 on Glossop Brook. There had been a former mill here in 1784. This building of 1870 closed in 1937 and was used for wartime storage and then remained derelict until it collapsed in 1954. The chimney was demolished two years later and the rest of the building was finally demolished in 1960 together with some terraced houses on the left. The new Methodist chapel, ambulance station and clinic were built on land near the old Palace Cinema on the corner of George Street and Chapel Street.

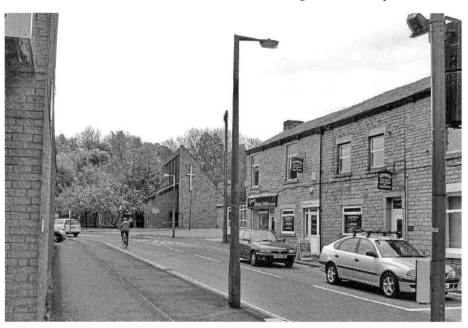

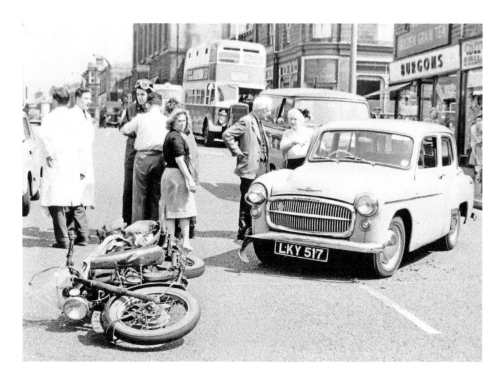

High Street West

High Street West in Glossop was the scene of a collision in June 1960 between a Hillman car and a motorcyclist. Only minor injuries were sustained but traffic, including the 125 Hyde to Manchester bus, was held up. Staff from the Mettrick's butchers, and other shops, were checking all was well with the motorcyclist, whose gear is very different from that worn by modern bikers. Burgons shop became a shoe shop and the rounded entrance was to the Newmarket Hotel, currently an optician as is the shop on the far right.

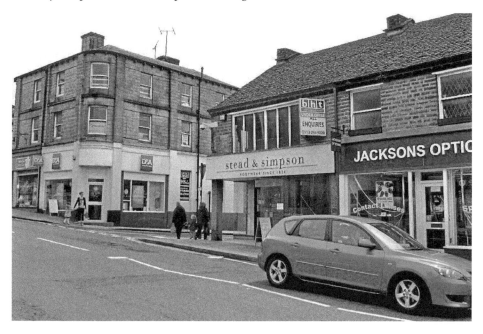

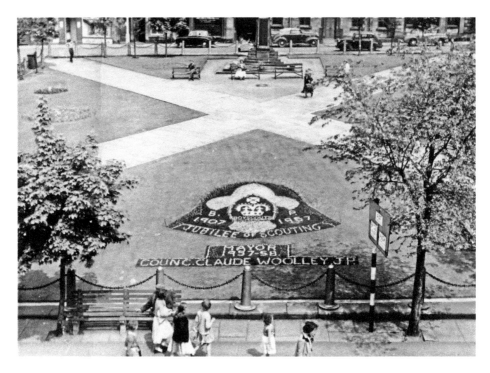

Norfolk Square

Glossop's Norfolk Square was once known as Norfolk Gardens. After the First World War, the daughter of Lord Doverdale, Mrs Bennett Sidebottom, financed the lawns and trees. Over the years, Norfolk Square has been laid out in many designs. In 1957, the carpet garden commemorated the Scouting Jubilee and the paths were laid diagonally. Today the paths lead up to the cenotaph, the Heritage Centre and shops on Henry Street. The following year the gardens heralded the visit of Charles Dutheil, the mayor from Millau, which became Glossop's twin town in France.

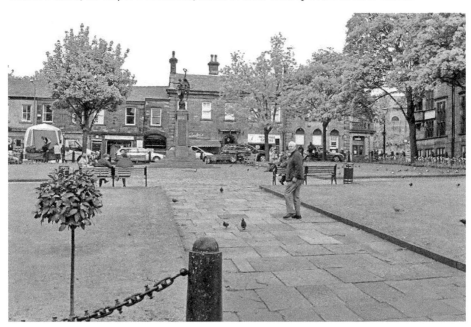

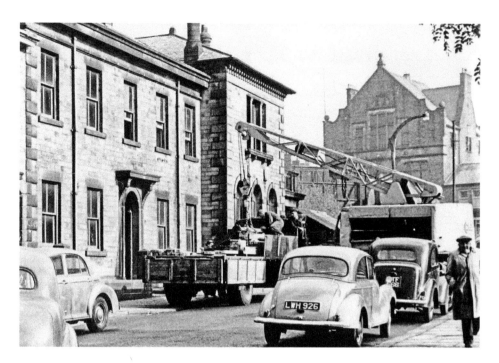

Bank House

Bank House on Henry Street, in Glossop, used to be the District Bank. In 1959, workers were removing the heavy safe by crane. The building became the Heritage and Tourist Information Centre and next-door Froggatt's used to sell floor coverings. At that time, parking on the streets was not a problem and most streets in the town had unrestricted parking. There is now a bus terminus at the end of the street. The imposing building on Norfolk Street is the Conservative Club.

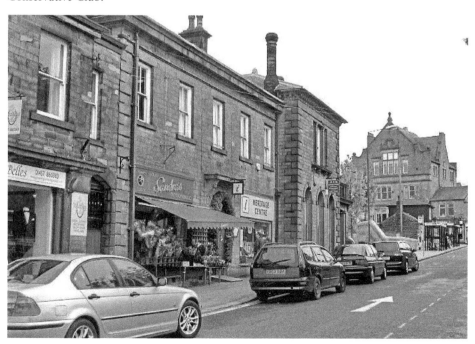

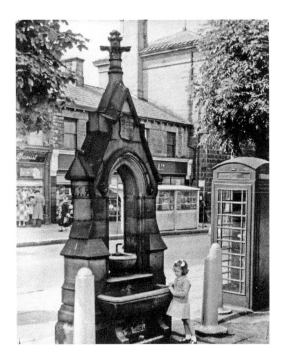

Glossop Drinking Fountain

The drinking fountain was given to Glossop by Mrs Wood, of the mill owning family, in 1881 along with another at Manor Park Road and a third at the top of Victoria Street. The top part was for humans to drink, the middle was for horses and the bottom was for dogs. In 1967, the council considered moving it but, with slight modifications, it still stands. The 'phone box has moved nearer to Norfolk Square, buses now stop lower down at the town hall. Woolworths, along with its stores in other towns, closed around the end of 2008 and the premises reopened as a frozen food shop the following year.

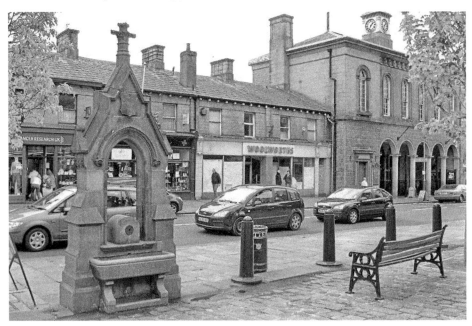

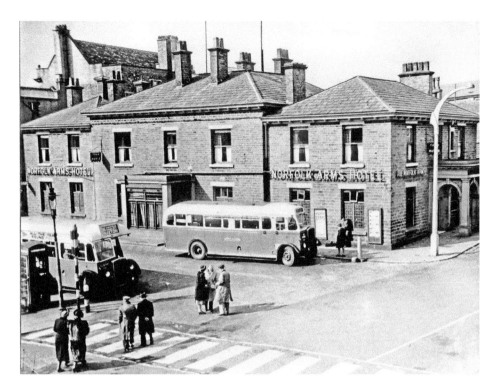

Norfolk Arms Hotel

In 1950, the licensee of the Norfolk Arms Hotel was Mr E. Smith. Originally, stagecoaches called here and horses were stabled at the back. For many years it was a bus terminus for single-decker buses on local routes and for the Buxton service. In 1964, it was proposed to pedestrianise High Street West from the Arundel Arms to Norfolk Arms. This never happened as is evident with the high volume of traffic that often queues to enter and depart from Glossop.

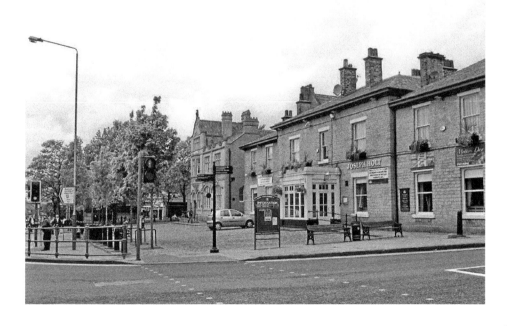

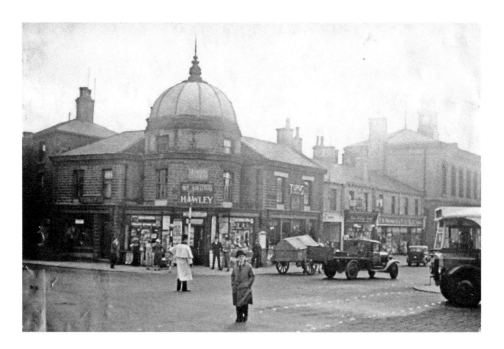

Hawley's Dome

Hawley's Dome was a prominent feature on the corner of High Street West and Victoria Street before it was demolished in 1937. The building became the HSBC bank next to Gregg's bakers, Finley McKinley's chemist became Cohen's and Woolworth's was to the right. Before traffic lights, police officers on point duty directed the assortment of vehicles including the horse drawn cart at this junction. Cars parked without restriction in front of the shops and most people wore hats!

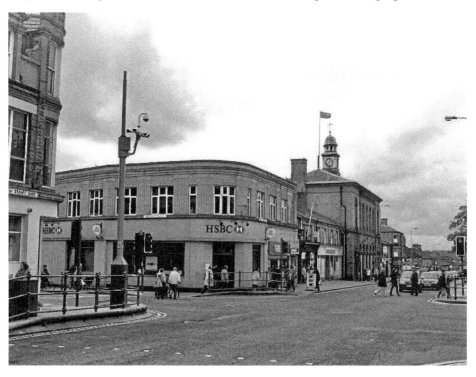

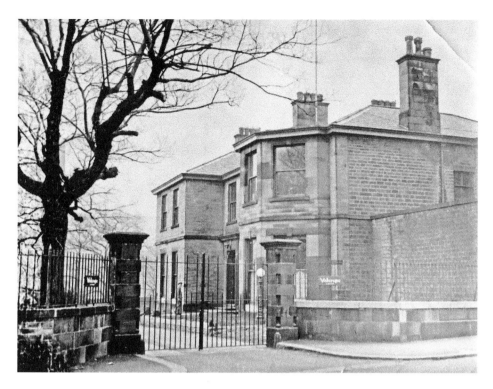

Easton House

Frances Sumner, who was Glossop's first mayor, built Easton House on High Street East, in 1857. It became the home of Lord Howard, but when the Howard's decided to leave Glossop for Yorkshire in the 1920s, the Glossop estates were sold to the local council. Easton House, together with its grounds and stables, was sold for £1,200. It became the offices for Volcrepe Ltd. and later E&R Polymers. In 1952, new gates were added, but in 2009 this once grand house and grounds are derelict and neglected. There are plans, however, for it to become part of the Manor House Surgery.

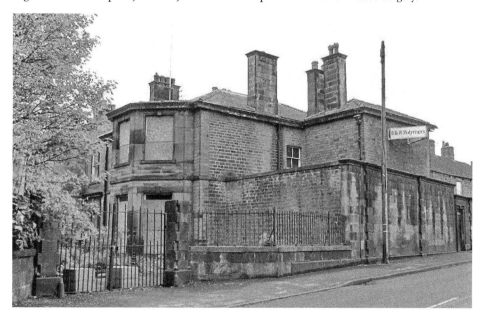

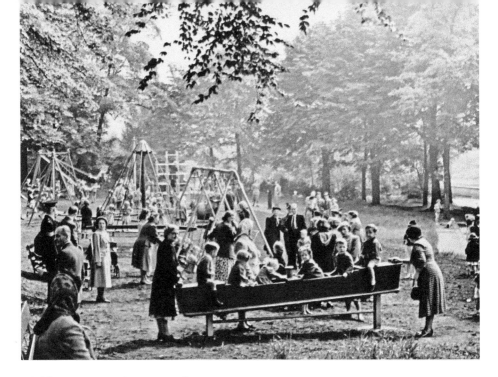

Children's Recreation Ground

The children's recreation ground in Manor Park has always been a popular location. The park opened to the public in 1927 and was originally the grounds of Glossop Hall, the home of Lord Howard the Duke of Norfolk. In 1951, £900 was spent to improve the play area and paddling pool, and Alderman Robert Boak, who was the mayor, gave it a second opening ceremony. Local children, parents and grandparents, as well as visitors from other towns, have always made for the park, especially at holiday times. Grannies no longer wear their best hats and the old metal umbrella and rocking boat have been replaced by up-to-date equipment that is still a great attraction for young people.

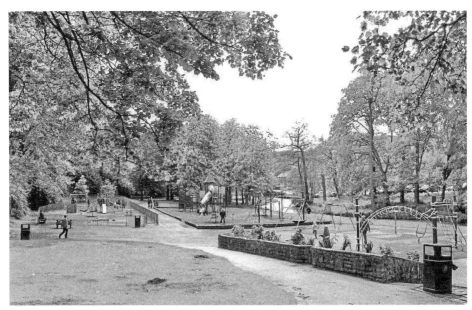

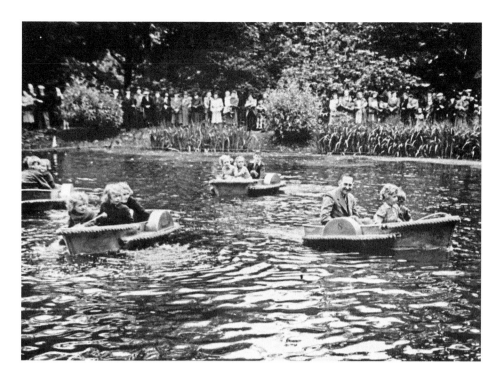

Manor Park

Amongst the park's attractions were a boating lake, an aviary and a pet's corner. It was a special treat, especially during the school holidays, for whole families to travel to Manor Park. In August 1947, large crowds always made for the boats that had to be propelled using one's hands. The boats were tied up in one corner of the pond overnight. Now ducks and other wild fowl have taken up residence, with a central island to nest on. When Manor Park was the garden of Glossop Hall, many acres of fine woodland were established.

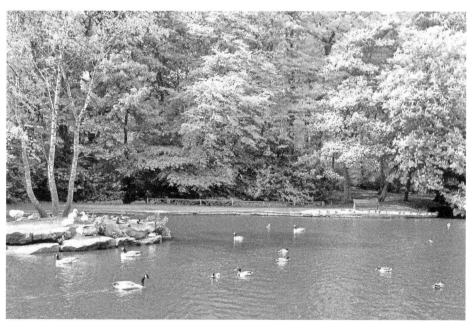

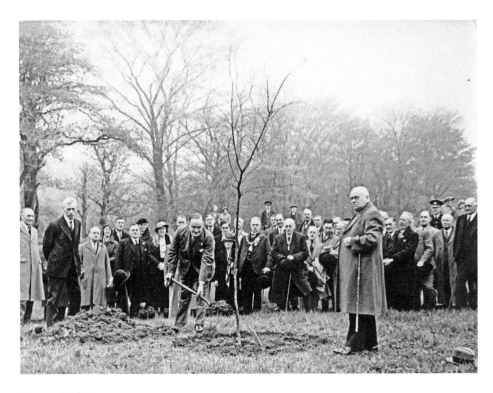

Manor Park Trees

The 'great and the good' have always gathered when notable events have taken place. Around 1936 Councillor Beckman was planting a tree in Manor Park with the mayor, Councillor J. Hague, together with other council members. Hats were doffed or laid on the ground for the one in whose memory they had gathered. Admired by several generations, the trees stand proud of the fact that years before others bothered to plant them for us to enjoy today. Today, hundred of fine trees make a splendid background to events such as the Glossop Car Show.

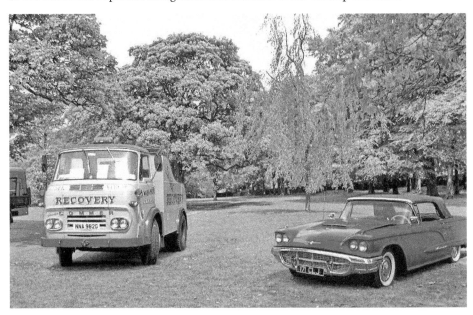

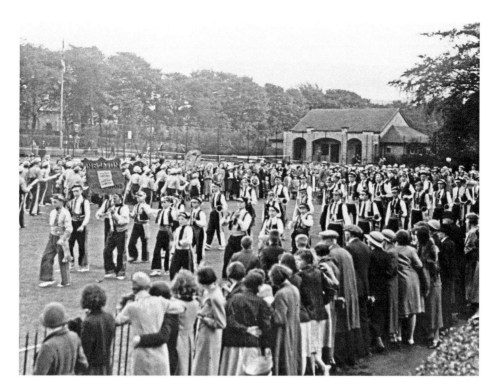

Manor Park Events

Hundreds of teams and young hopefuls have played tennis matches since the courts were opened to the public, many trophies have been received and freezer's full of ice cream have been sold at the pavilion. Since Manor Park was opened in 1927, there have been carnivals, bonfire celebrations and many other special days held within its gates. In the 1930s, large crowds watched this Jazz Band from Newton. Glossop's Carnival still parades to the park in the summer months. A miniature railway takes passengers large and small around a winding track starting by the side of the tennis courts.

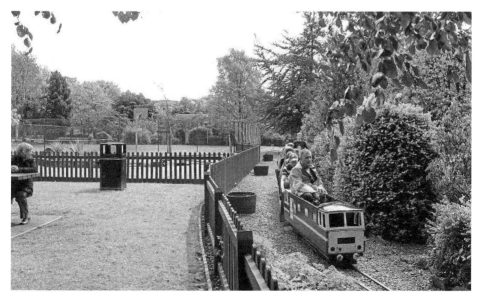

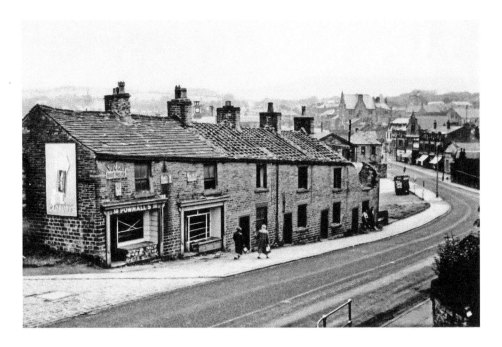

Shivering Row

A row of four houses and two shops once stood on Victoria Street, in Glossop. They became known as Shivering Row after being struck by lightening in 1862. By August 1957, after standing empty for some time, they were being demolished due to the walls bulging. Pownall's shop had moved to premises on High Street East. The Telephone Exchange was built behind these properties in 1960. Over the roofs, the town hall clock pokes out between the chimneys. The gategouse of Wood's Mill, built in 1780, is on the right. The mill itself has since become Howard Town Mill appartments.

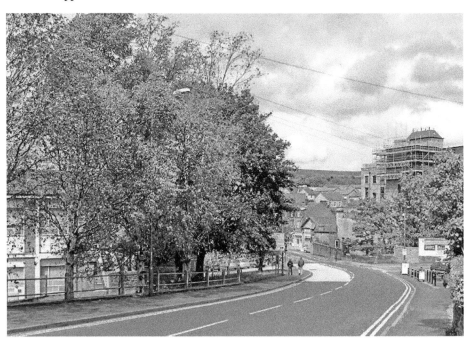

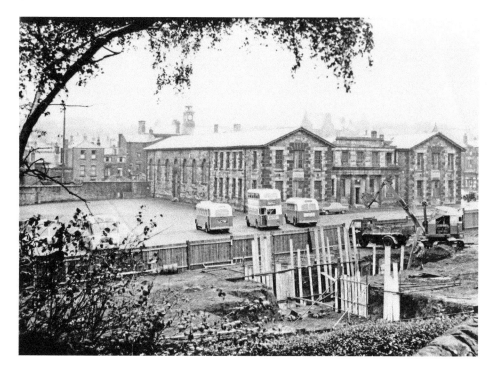

Glossop Town Hall and Market Ground

The No. 127 Hadfield bus, some coaches and single-decker buses used to terminate on the Market Ground next to Glossop's town hall. Before 1838, the site was a field called The Platt, owned by the proprietor of The Tontine that became the Norfolk Arms. The mayor opened the new Telephone Exchange in February 1960. The North Western Road Car Company opened a bus depot on York Street after they took over from the Urban Electric Supply Co. Ltd. when the tramway from Glossop to Hadfield was abandoned in 1927. Buses no longer stop on the Market Ground but use the High Street and Henry Street. Market stalls and public toilets fill the space to the left and cars and taxis parks on the remainder.

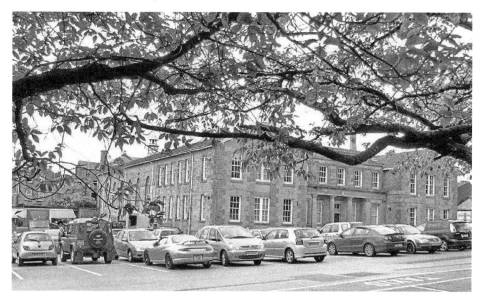

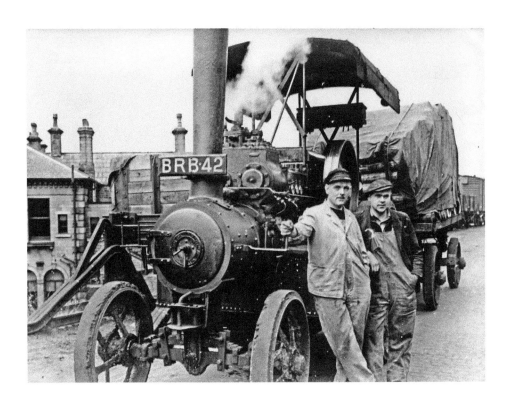

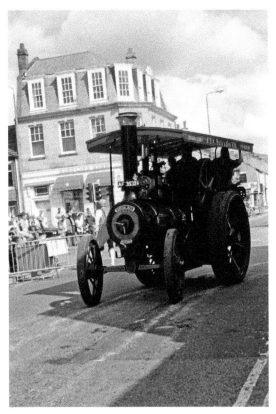

Traction Engines at Glossop

From the 1800s, William Olive and Edward Partington built up a papermaking complex in Glossop called Turn Lee Mills. The side of the railway station stacked logs for use in these mills before being transported under tarpaulin in wagons pulled by traction engines. George Wilmot and Tom Hinchliff were the drivers of *Joan* in 1951. For many years, Glossop has hosted a Victorian Weekend where its people and entertainers dress and recreate the past. In the grand parade, clog dancers, street entertainers and old vehicles are some of the attractions that draw the crowds to wallow in a bit of nostalgia.

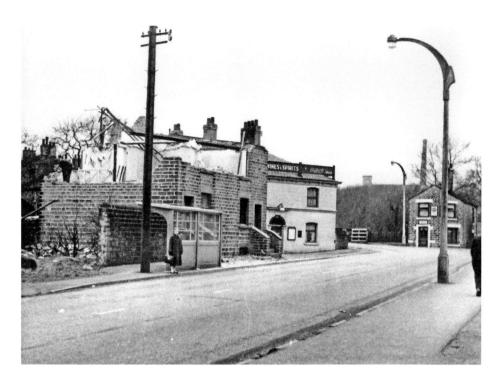

Woolley Bridge

Woolley Bridge over the River Etherow marks the boundary between Derbyshire and Cheshire. The small building on the right, originally the Toll House, became a sweet and ice cream shop before being turned into a private house. The white building was the Spread Eagle public house, later becoming The Riverside. The houses in front were demolished in 1959 to make a larger car park. At this busy junction, now with a mini roundabout, the pub stands boarded up and the buses to Hyde and Ashton no longer stop at this point.

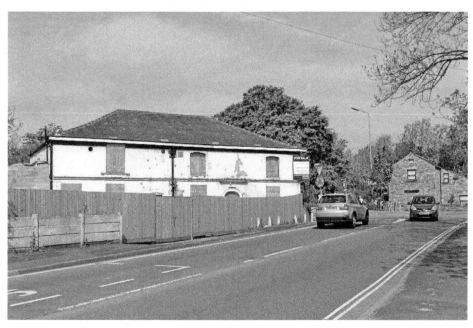

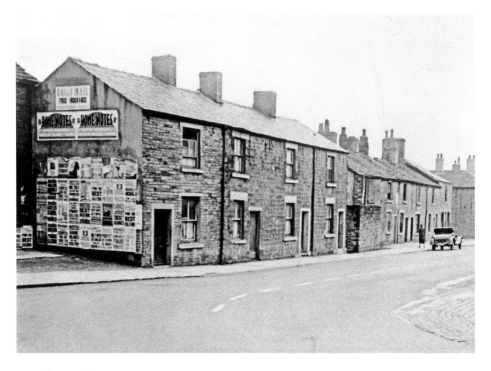

Woolley Bridge

On the other side of the road at Woolley Bridge stood a row of houses whose gable end displayed billboards for Middleton's shop to the left. The newsagent's has become a private dwelling and the houses were demolished in the 1940s. The side road in front of the car was Lees Row, where one of the houses was used as a Mission Hall for St Andrew's church in Hadfield. The site became a service centre for Glossop Caravans and premises of Travis Perkins.

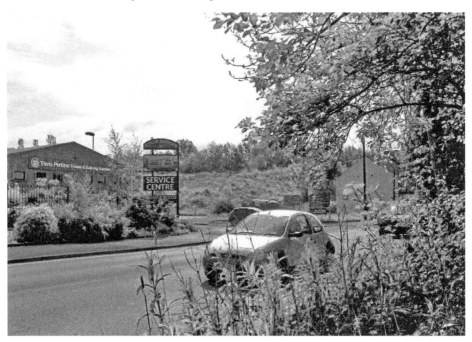

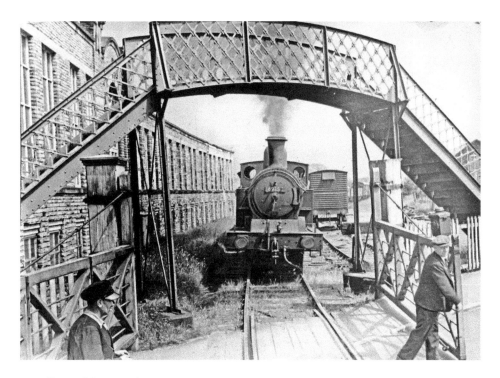

Woolley Bridge Road

The Manchester, Sheffield & Lincolnshire Railway Company opened a branch line in 1879 to transport goods to and from the mills built along the River Etherow. Traffic was stopped across Woolley Bridge Road as gates were opened to allow the trains to pass. At such times, pedestrians had to use the wooden footbridge over the line. The last freight train (69353) on this route completed its final journey in June 1951 with Guard Jim Plant and Shunter William Hall. The line finally closed in 1964 and the footbridge came down two years later. A new housing development, Etherow Walk, was built nearby and the track now forms part of the Longdendale Trail.

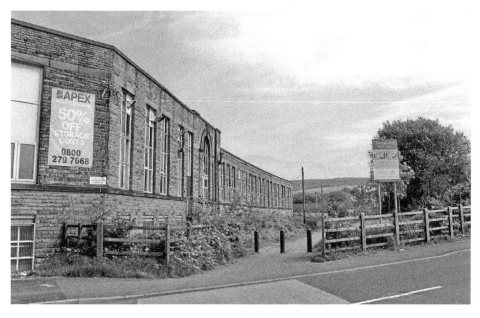

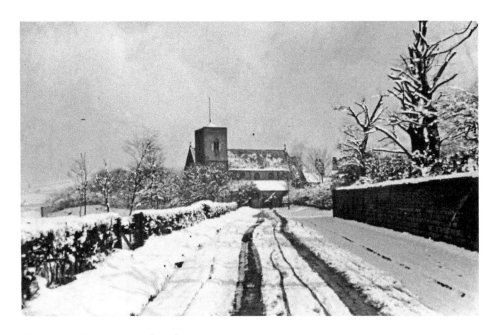

St Charles' Borromeo church

St Charles' Borromeo church was opened in 1858 at the end of The Carriage Drive, in Hadfield by Lord Edward Fitzalan Howard a former Duke of Norfolk. Glossop Hall, the home of the Howards, was used for Roman Catholic worship before any churches were built in the area. The surrounding land was purchased by Manchester City Council to move residents in poor housing in the Manchester districts of Gorton, Miles Platting and Openshaw. The houses were built in 1962 and most of the new tenants paid rents of just £2 per week.

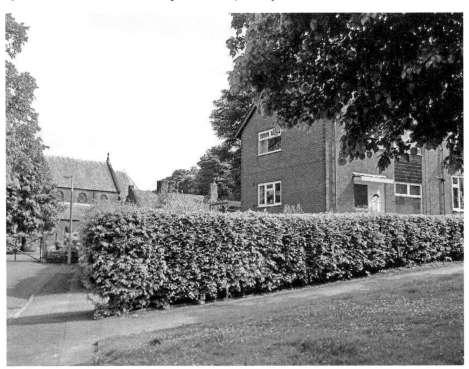

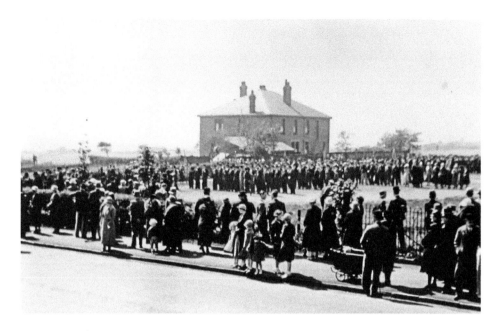

Mersey Bank House

Mersey Bank House was built by local mill owners on the corner of The Carriage Drive and Chapel Lane, Hadfield, in around 1855. John and Edward Platt lived there in 1907 and Ernest Wilman resided there in the 1930s when this large gathering of the local gentry, in their bowler hats, assembled. In 1959, the Minister of Housing & Local Government approved a compulsory order on 25 acres of land surrounding the house to built 290 overspill homes, which were built in the 1960s. Mersey Bank became a Nursing Home & Young Disabled Unit run by Cregmoor Healthcare.

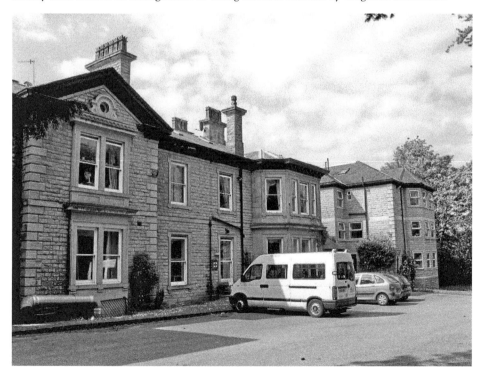

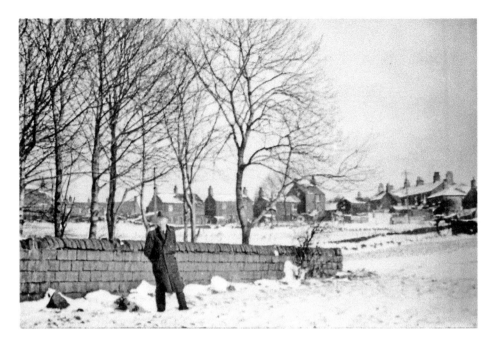

Chapel Lane, Hadfield

Chapel Lane, Hadfield, was named after a Methodist chapel built in 1804 by mill owner John Thornley at a cost of £200. In 1958 Harry Buxton, whose collection of old photographs form the basis of this book, was standing by the walls of the graveyard. Today, it can be found next to the infant school on Mersey Bank Road, but its high walls have gone. It was last used for burials in 1859 and most of the graves lie flat among the grass but the headstone in memory of John & Mary Banker still stands. The houses on Old Hall Square and Hadfield Road are now hidden by the newer housing estate.

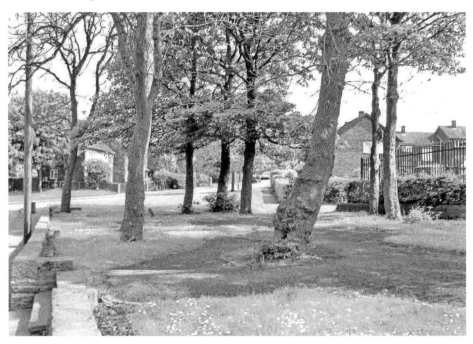

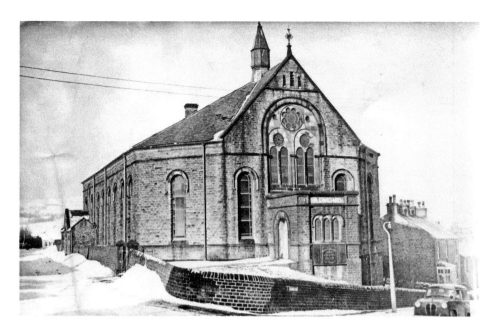

The Wesleyan Chapel

The Wesleyan chapel stood on the corner of Bank Street and Paradise Street, in Hadfield. It opened in 1878 and amalgamated with Woolley Bridge Road Methodists in 1963. At its closure in 1996 the congregation, led by Reverend Hazel Cooke, processed to new premises on Station Road. The eldest member of the chapel, Phyllis Harrison, cut the ribbon at the opening ceremony. One year later, the old chapel was destroyed by fire and demolished. New housing now occupies the site that is aptly named Church View.

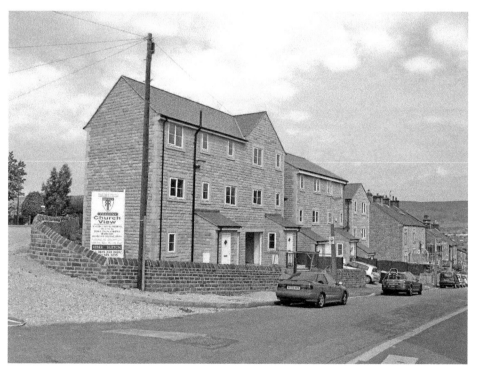

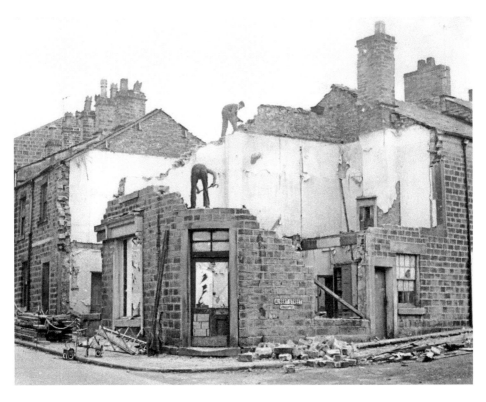

Albert Street and Station Road

The Radio Retailers, in Hadfield, was formerly a chemist's shop on the corner of Albert Street and Station Road. It was demolished in May 1960 without the aid of scaffolding as each stone was knocked to the ground using just a crowbar and balancing skills! The unadopted street has now become a car park. Willow Bank Residential Home stands higher up the street on the opposite side. Hadfield became 'Royston Vasey' in the satirical television series *The League Of Gentleman;* the opening shot was of Bleaklow, the hill that overlooks the village.

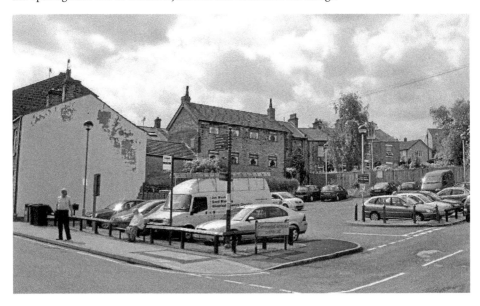

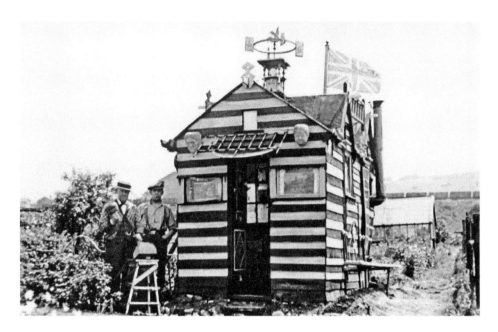

Padfield Main Road

At the end of Lambgates, off Station Road in Hadfield, open land led to Padfield Main Road. Allotments, hen cotes and pigeon lofts used some of this land, known as Roughfields, whilst animals grazed on the remainder. During the war, when Britain was encouraged to 'Dig for Victory', Mr Gill had turned his allotment shed into a kind of patriotic 'Heath Robinson' shelter proudly flying the Union Jack. Housing has now been built on some of the land. The goods wagons on the railway line bound for Woodhead Tunnel were passing in the distance.

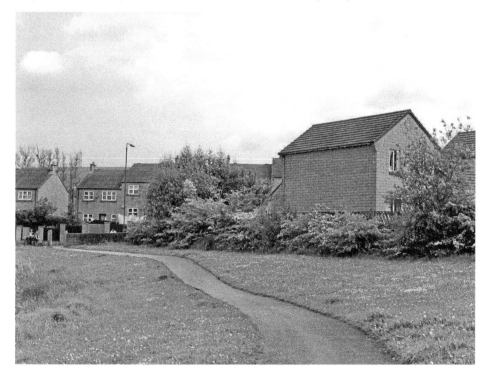

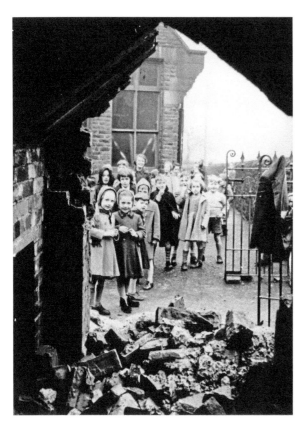

St Andrew's School

St Andrew's C of E junior school in Hadfield was financed with voluntary contributions and erected in 1855. Air raid shelters had stood in the playground since wartime but in December 1957, watched by some of the younger pupils, they were being demolished after they were thought to be unsafe. Some years later, after the school moved to the former Castle Secondary School on Hadfield Road, Kingsmoor private school took over the premises. It is now the Red Dragon Cantonese Restaurant.

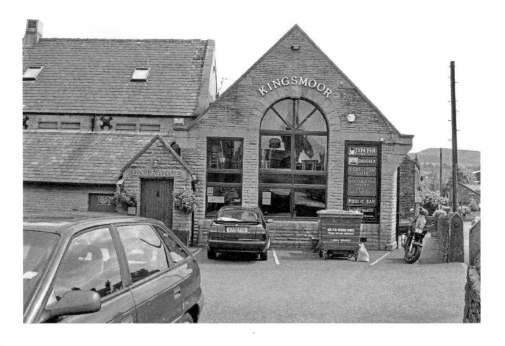

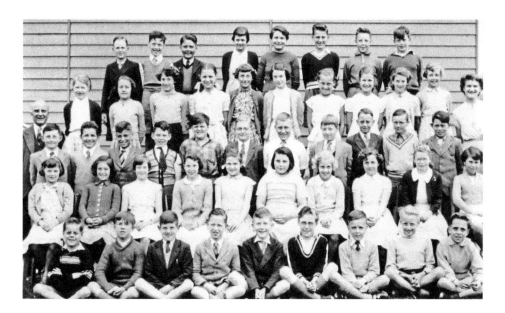

St Andrew's School Reunion

Children from Standard 4 at St Andrew's School in 1957 with Headmaster Mr Bowden and class teacher Miss Child. With forty-eight pupils in the class, these children were taught away from the main school in two Medway wooden classrooms built the previous year on the playing fields behind Castle School. Forty-five years later most of the class met up at a reunion organized by former pupil Marjorie Dean, at their old school. The line up was not as formal and many could only recognize their former classmates from the identity name and photo around their necks! All were delighted that their first teacher, Mrs Peggy Davies, was able to attend.

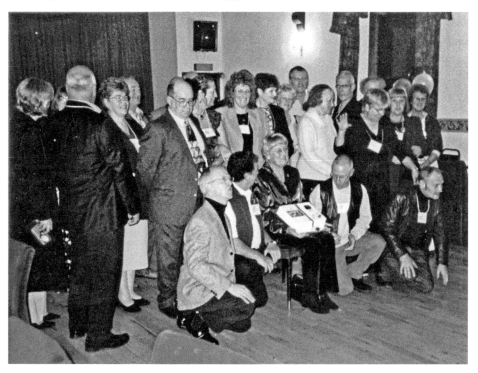

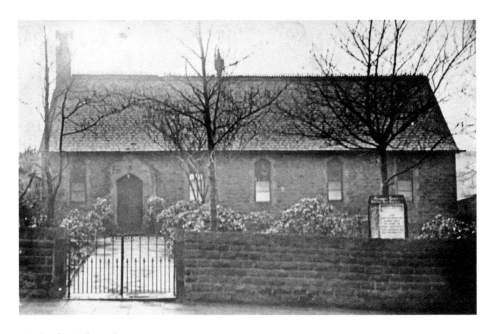

Methodist Chapel

The increased number of births after the Second World War meant that the local schools became overcrowded. These children, known as 'baby boomers', had to walk after morning assembly in St Andrew's School to other premises for their lessons. One classroom was in the Methodist chapel on Station Road, Hadfield. Many years later, the building has been extended and is the Carmel Christian Centre.

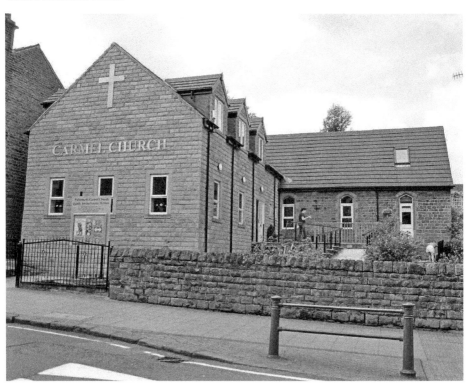

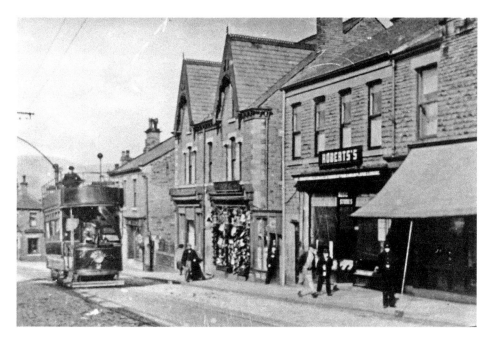

Station Road

Trams ran from Old Glossop to Hadfield from 1903 to 1927. The journey up to the Palatine Hotel, on Station Road in Hadfield, cost just two old pennies. In 1904, 20,000 passengers were using this route and the loop line from Glossop to Whitfield each week. Motor buses started to run from 1926. A century later, cars and buses now park and travel where the tramlines once stood, pedestrians no longer walk in their clogs to the mills and many of the shops, with their sun awnings, have become private homes.

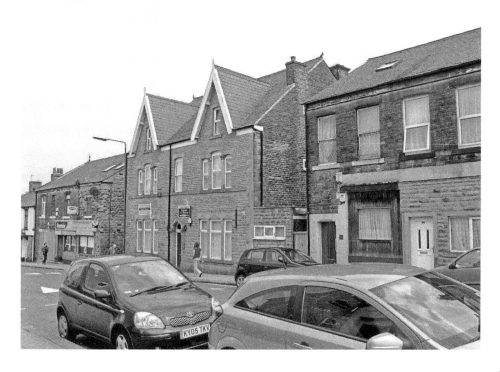

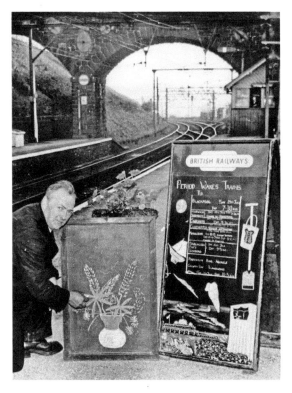

Hadfield Railway Station

Hadfield Railway Station won several awards for best-kept and tidiest station in the 1950s when it had a beautiful floral garden on the platform. During the local Wakes Week when many of the mills, factories and shops closed for the annual holidays, British Rail provided steam trains to the seaside for locals to get away. In 1956, the porter, Mr H. Tongue, used his artistic skills to advertise some of these special trains. The signal box at the far end was moved to the other end of the platform. Since the demise of the line to Sheffield, there is only the need for one platform and one booking clerk.

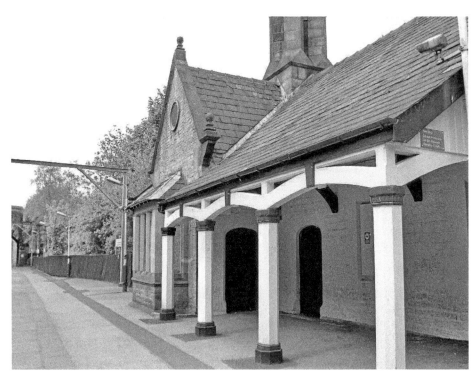

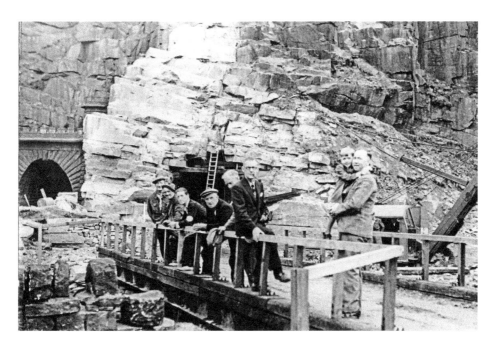

The Woodhead Tunnel

Steam trains carrying goods from Manchester via Penistone en route to Sheffield, used to travel through Hadfield Station and the Woodhead Tunnel. There were two tunnels before a third was started around 1949 for the use of electrified locomotives. Photographer Harry Buxton and members of his family chatted to workers taking a break from their work. Alan Lennox-Boyd, the Minister of Transport & Civil Aviation, opened the new tunnel on 3 June 1954. The line closed in 1981, and the route from Hadfield to the tunnel became the six mile-long Longdendale Trail that forms part of the 210 mile-long Trans Pennine Trail for walkers, cyclists and horses.

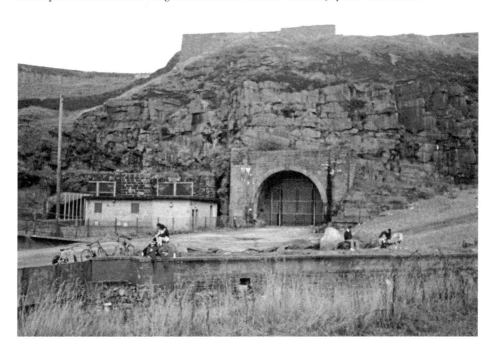

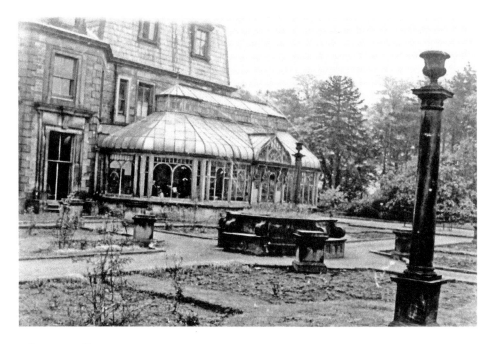

Glossop Hall

Glossop Hall was the home of the Dukes of Norfolk up to 1927, when Lord Howard moved from the town. In September 1949 it was sold to Kingsmoor School who used it until July 1956, but some three years later the hall was demolished. The land was sold for building and bungalows were built on the site where the Howards once resided. When St Andrew's School in Hadfield had vacated their building, it was used for several years by Kingsmoor School.

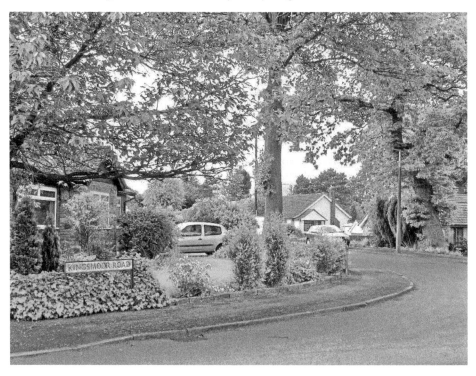

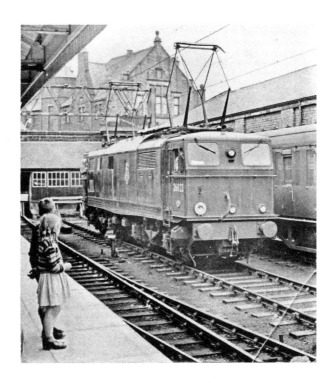

Glossop Railway Station

The branch line, from Dinting to Glossop, was financed by Henry Charles Howard, the 13th duke of Norfolk. After the Manchester-Sheffield & Lincolnshire Railway Company refused to build the line, he had it built to ensure there was ample coal for the cotton mills, because the local supply was insufficient. The duke also built the station at Glossop, which is now Grade II listed. Above the entrance he placed a stone lion, representing his coat of arms, at a cost of £37 10s. Electric trains superseded the steam trains from 1953 when the platform was on the opposite side from the engine shed, now part of the Co-operative Society superstore.

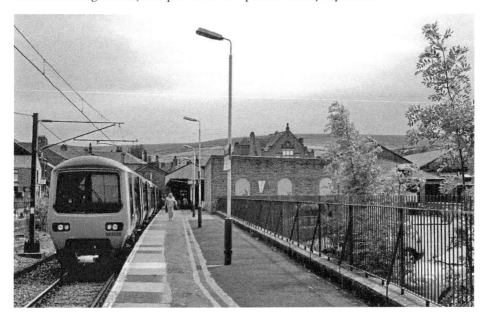

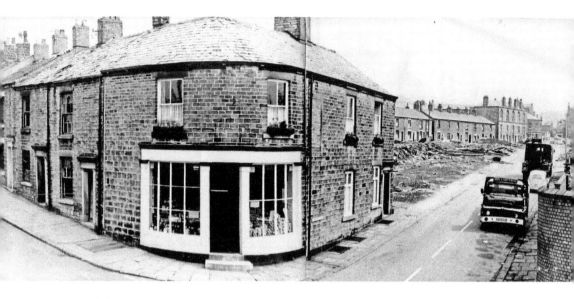

Arundel House

Many of the streets in the centre of Glossop bear names relating to the Howard family who were the dukes of Norfolk. In the 1960s, houses on Bernard Street and Arundel Street were demolished, making room for a car park on Edward Street. Arundel House, built around the corner of Arundel Street and Bernard Street, has been tastefully restored from a corner shop. The grime from days before smokeless fuels has been cleaned to show off the stone so typical of buildings in the area. Looking towards Henry Street in the distance, the old three-storey Liberal Hall still stands.

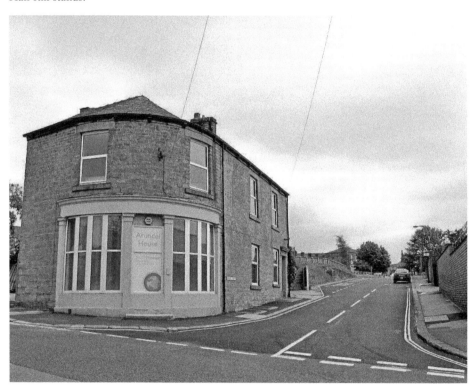

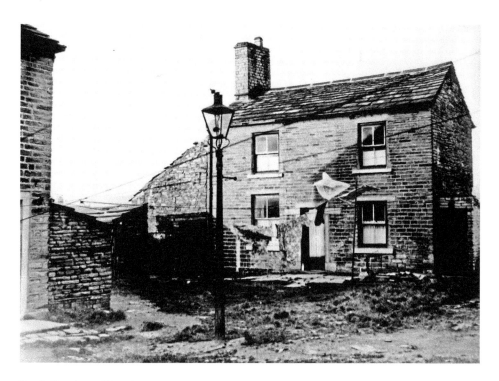

Back Kershaw Street

These old houses on Back Kershaw Street stood in the Whitfield district of Glossop. The toilet was housed outside at the side of this house with its neat net curtains at the sash windows. In 1961, the daily milk delivery stood on the doorstep and windy conditions caused the washing to wind around the line, held up by a rather tall prop. Could it have once been the 'knocker-up's pole' used at the windows to get people out of their beds for early morning work? The scene, lit by a gas lamp, changed after demolition in April 1967, and new terraced housing is now evident on Kershaw Street.

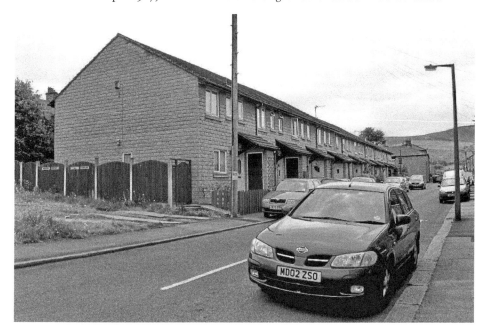

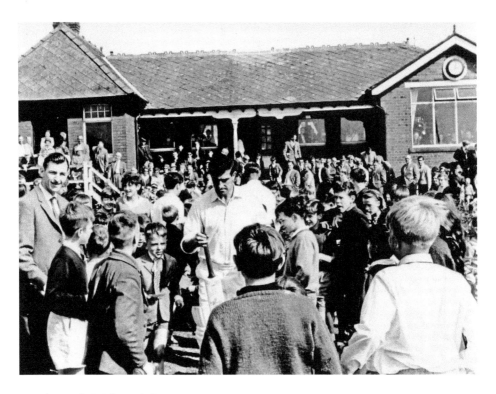

North Road Cricket Club

Glossop has several cricket grounds, but in 1964, Frederick Sewards Truman, born in 1931 and better known as Freddie, brought out great crowds when he appeared at North Road Cricket Club. His many fans, of all ages, turned out to watch him play. He was a skilled fast bowler who took 307 test wickets in his career. Ladybower Court retirement homes have been built overlooking the grounds and a new clubhouse was completed in 2008.

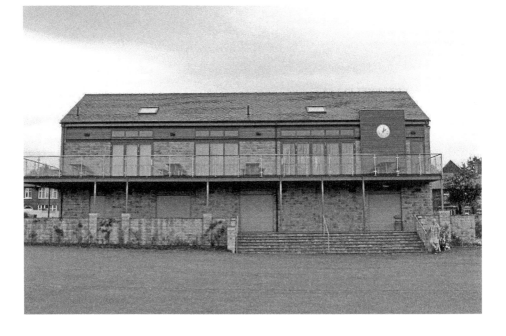

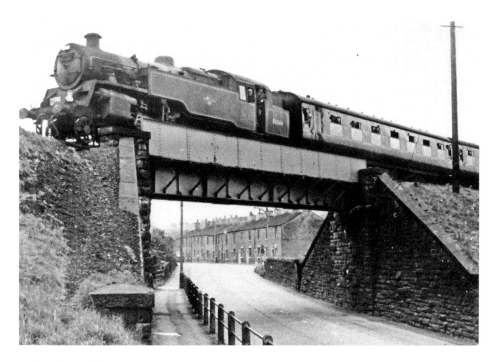

Melandra Bridge

Melandra Bridge at Brookfield, Glossop, was built in 1886 and named after a Roman Fort of 78 AD that stood nearby. The bridge formed part of the Waterside branch line that conveyed freight to the mills along the River Etherow. The last goods train passed over the bridge in February 1964 but in 1965 a train trip for enthusiasts made the journey. This area, near the Spring Tavern Inn, had been the scene of many floods so after the line closed, the level of the road was raised and the bridge was demolished in March 1966. Now the route forms part of the Transpennine bridlepath where equestrians have their own set of traffic lights to cross the busy A57.

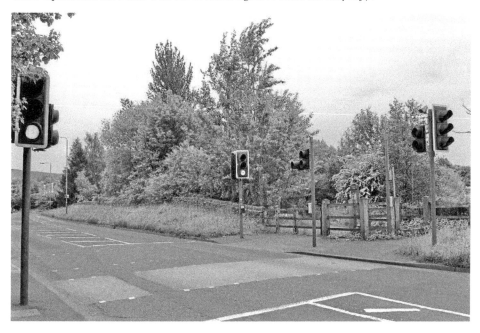

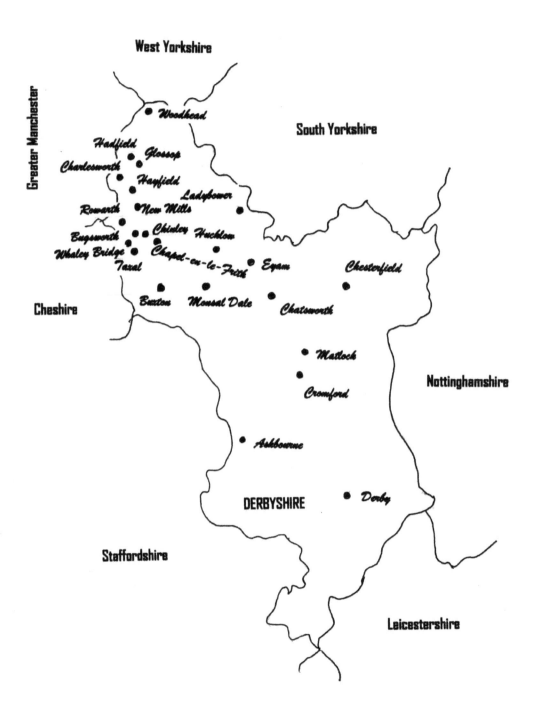

West Yorkshire

Greater Manchester

South Yorkshire

Woodhead

Hadfield
Glossop
Charlesworth
Hayfield
Ladybower
Rowarth
New Mills
Bugsworth
Chinley
Hucklow
Whaley Bridge
Chapel-en-le-Frith
Eyam
Chesterfield
Taxal

Cheshire

Buxton
Monsal Dale
Chatsworth

Matlock

Cromford

Nottinghamshire

Ashbourne

DERBYSHIRE
Derby

Staffordshire

Leicestershire